I0805100

BENNINGTON VANGUARDS

BENNINGTON VANGUARDS

Pioneers and Poets

BILL MORGAN & TOM FELS

THE History PRESS

Published by The History Press,
An imprint of Arcadia Publishing
Charleston, SC
www.historypress.com

First published 2025

Manufactured in the United States

ISBN 9781467158541

Library of Congress Control Number: 2025931877

Notice: The information in this book is true and complete to the best of our knowledge. It is offered without guarantee on the part of the authors or The History Press. The authors and The History Press disclaim all liability in connection with the use of this book.

For Jennifer and Judy.

CONTENTS

ACKNOWLEDGEMENTS

First and foremost, I would like to express my gratitude to Tom Fels for his work bringing this history to light back in 1999. Tom has long been a font of information about Bennington, and he has freely given his time consulting on this new book. He graciously consented to have his work expanded on, and any errors that arise from my meddling are certainly no fault of his. His continuing support in this project is greatly appreciated, and the resulting volume could never have been completed without him.

Callie Raspuzzi, the curator of the Bennington Museum's collections, has been a fabulous source of help and information. Without her contributions, this book would have been impossible. Not only did she provide most of the illustrations for the book, but she also wrote the text for the sections on Native Americans and Margaret Bowen. Her knowledge and enthusiasm helped make certain that no group was left out of this history.

A subcommittee from the Bennington Historical Society and Bennington Museum has given freely of their time and energy to advise and consult on the preparation of this book as well. Special appreciation is due to those members: Joe Hall, Martin Mahoney, Callie Raspuzzi and Tyler Resch.

In the course of this work, we have been aided by a legion of local historians and institutions, and without their knowledge and suggestions, this volume would not have been as accurate or interesting as it is. We thank them all without reservations.

Everyone at the Bennington Museum has been instrumental in creating this book, which we hope is both informative and attractive. The museum's staff, along with historical society members, have helped make certain that Bennington's past will always be remembered. Nearly all the individuals who are featured within this book have been the subjects of programs and lectures presented by the society and the museum. Thanks are due to all those members, past and present, who had a hand in bringing their stories to life.

Of the many people and institutions who have assisted in one way or another in this continuing project, we would like to single out the following for especially meritorious service:

At the Bennington Historical Society: Anne Bugbee, Charles Dewey, Robert Ebert, Joe Hall, Jackie Marro, Don Miller, David Pilachowski, Tyler Resch, Dawn and Ray Rodrigues and Bob Tegart.

At the Bennington Museum: Jamie Franklin, Ruth Levin, Martin Mahoney, Deana Mallory, Steve Miller and Callie Raspuzzi.

At the Bennington Free Library, we would like to thank the director, Lynne Fonteneau McCann, as well as the librarians and the volunteers in the library's History Room for their indispensable aid.

Tordis Isselhardt at Bennington's Images from the Past has supplied many key photographs and insights.

From the town of Bennington and the Bicenquinquagenary Committee: Stuart Hurd, Joseph Parks and Jonah Spivak.

At the *Bennington Banner*, past and present: Jordan Brechenser, Darrell Byne, Joseph Karius, Stephanie Lupa, Erin McKenny, Jules Molenda, Mary Rogers, Mark Rondeau, Robin Smith and Cathy Vosburgh.

And of course, it almost goes without saying that Bennington's citizens at large have provided us with counsel and valuable historical information. Thanks go to Ned Dewey, Phil Holland, Tony Marro, Stephen Perkins, Jane Radocchia, Cindy Smith and Gail Wiese of the Vermont Historical Society.

To the many others who offered illustrations and advice or assisted in clarifying the history or the text, we offer our sincerest thanks and hope the effort represented here is worthy of the time and energy they so generously contributed.

And to the editors and staff of The History Press, their interest and expertise made it all possible. Special thanks to Mike Kinsella and Ashley Hill for guiding us through the maze of publication.

Finally, our gratitude goes to our unsung muses of history Jennifer Fels and Judy Matz.

Bill Morgan
Bennington, VT
2024

It is a pleasure to report that proceeds from the sale of this book benefit the Bennington Museum and Bennington Historical Society.

INTRODUCTION

Twenty-five years ago, to commemorate the 250th anniversary of the signing of Bennington's charter in 1749, Tom Fels, the *Bennington Banner*, the town of Bennington and the Bicenquinquagenary Committee joined to publish a pamphlet containing a brief history of the town and its residents. In honor of the 250th anniversary of the Battle of Bennington, it seems appropriate to update and expand those biographical sketches for a new generation.

> *Almost every Benningtonian realizes that the first real commercial and social village in Bennington was located where the Battle Monument stands today, and that downtown Bennington grew up in the early 1800s, passing the older village in size and importance. A smaller number realize that the older village was on hard times in the latter half of the 1880s, until the Battle Monument was built, after which it changed into a summer colony and then an attractive suburb. But how did it happen that the first village was planted—or did it simply spring up?—in Old Bennington? Reasons of military defense, or fear of disease, or the existence of a natural clearing among the trees? Or could the site have been chosen to comply with Governor Benning Wentworth's mandate to build the commercial center on a sixty-four-acre site located at the center of the town of Bennington? For Old Bennington, believe it or not, is exactly in the center of the town.*
>
> *For background, it should be kept in mind that New Hampshire's Governor Benning Wentworth divided up the six-square-mile town he*

> *named after himself into sixty-four squares of three hundred and twenty acres. Each owner of a square ("right," as a square of land was called) also owned a corresponding one-acre square in the sixty-four-acre Town Plot supposedly located in the center of the town. The map which Benning Wentworth caused to be drawn to accompany his grant of the lands in 1749 shows the shape of the plot as six-sided. There is some evidence that the early Benningtonians set out to honor Wentworth's orders, because some of the early deeds to lands in the four rights which touched the center show that those squares were short by sixteen acres each of the three hundred and twenty acres they should contain, and the perimeter descriptions of some of the deeds show the missing part to be in the shape of one-fourth of a six-sided plot, just as would be expected.*

This quotation was from an article written in 1981 by Charles G. Bennett, the librarian emeritus of the Bennington Museum, titled "A Record of Our Land." It serves as an explanation of how the land was parceled out, but what wasn't pointed out was that none of the original purchasers of the "rights" ever settled on their property or even saw the land they bought. They drew lots for their parcels of sixty-four acres each and were simply investors who then divided and sold acreage to the later pioneers who first came to the area in 1761. Thus, the town of Bennington began completely on speculation.

NATIVE AMERICANS

People were living on the land that is now Bennington for thousands of years before white settlers arrived. Archaeologists have excavated a Late Archaic settlement on the banks of the Walloomsac near the present-day Silk Road covered bridge that dates to around 2,000 BCE. Arrowheads and other stone tools have been found in other locations. These first people were likely the ancestors of the Mohican, who call themselves *Muh-he-con-ne-ok*, "the people of the waters that are never still." Their ancient ancestors may have been here for as many as six thousand years before that. Unfortunately, no documents remain to tell the story of individual Native Americans. Some of our roads were no doubt originally mere paths made by the Natives who tracked their prey through the forests. Place names have also been handed down from earlier inhabitants and recorded only verbally. The names of whoever called this place home before Samuel Robinson happened upon the valley in the mid-eighteenth century will always remain a mystery, but they were here.

Native groups in New England lived highly flexible, fluid and opportunistic lifestyles that revolved around the woodlands where they hunted and farmed. Their society appears to have been organized into small core communities that were then linked to family groups. They grew crops, including corn, squash and beans, and moved seasonally to take advantage of foraging, hunting grounds and fishing spots. They managed forests, which provided them with abundant fruits, nuts and wild game.

Native American stone mortar and other implements found in Bennington County. *Bennington Museum, Bennington, VT.*

The arrival of Europeans brought disease, for which Native people had no immunities, and as a result, their populations were decimated. This, in turn, caused massive social upheaval. Early Dutch traders developed relationships with the Mohican, including at trading posts in Hoosick and White Creek, New York. Traders encouraged Native men to hunt beaver exclusively, offering guns, new tools, cloth and iron kettles in exchange. These new trading partners encouraged Native communities to give up their traditional relationships with the land in favor of gathering as many beaver pelts as possible. It was not a sustainable lifestyle, and communities that were already traumatized by epidemics faced further pressure to assimilate.

New York government officials, in the 1600s, invited local Natives to settle in Schaghticoke to form a buffer between them and the French and their Native allies. In 1738, the Mohicans gave Reverend John Sergeant permission to start a mission that became the village of Stockbridge, Massachusetts. Many moved to that town to take advantage of its church and school. Other Native people migrated north and joined the Catholic communities allied with the French. We do not know whether people from Vermont were among either group, but when white settlers arrived in Bennington in 1761, they did not record any Native people living in the immediate region.

In 1767, a group of Mohicans, including Captain Jacobs and others, challenged English settlers' ownership of the land in the recent New Hampshire Grants. They claimed that they alone owned title to the land in southern Vermont granted by New Hampshire's Royal Governor Benning Wentworth. A group of 101 settlers came together to assess the Mohicans' claims, and on November 30, 1767, they appointed Reverend Jedediah Dewey, Captain John Fassett and Stephen Fay to negotiate for clear title (at the time, their titles were also threatened by New York claimants). There is no known account of the result of that meeting. Stephen Fay at least continued to deal with Mohican men. His ledger includes an account for Captain Solomon Uhhaunauwaunmut, whom he recorded in his account book in 1771 and 1772. Captain Solomon was chief sachem of the Stockbridge Mohicans and a prominent community leader, diplomat, military captain and orator.

The Mohicans worked closely with white leaders in the American colonies during the American Revolution. In early 1775, Captain Solomon declared that the Mohicans would fight with the Patriots and that they would also encourage the Mohawks and Haudenosaunee to side with them as well. In return, he expected the new American government would help his people defend their just rights from white settler encroachment. Captain Solomon led a company of Mohican soldiers in the Battle of Bunker Hill in 1775. He died in February 1777, but later that year, Mohican men from Stockbridge fought on the side of the Patriots in the Battle of Saratoga (they arrived too late to assist at the Battle of Bennington).

When the surviving Mohican warriors returned home, they discovered that their lands in Stockbridge were lost through mortgage and debt, often through fraudulent means, and that plans had already been made to remove them from Stockbridge. The American government repeatedly broke its promises to Native allies after the war. After a series of forced migrations, these Natives now live in Wisconsin as the Stockbridge-Munsee band of Mohican Indians.

BENNING WENTWORTH

1696–1770

Bennington was named for and by Benning Wentworth, the first royal governor of New Hampshire, who had been appointed to that position by the Crown in 1741. He was born in 1696 in Portsmouth, which was then part of the colony of Massachusetts. His father and grandfather were both wealthy Portsmouth merchants; his father, John, was lieutenant governor under Governor Jonathan Belcher of Massachusetts. Benning was a 1715 graduate of Harvard, and his raucous and ill-mannered undergraduate life set the tone for his later career. Among other transgressions at school, he reportedly set a record for breaking windows. Later, he joined the family business of trading in wines and spirits, as well as timber, munitions and other commodities. Wentworth's family was especially prominent in the lumber business, and in 1743, Benning was appointed surveyor of the king's forests in North America, charged with administering the White Pine Laws. These laws stipulated that all trees of a certain size must be reserved for use as masts for the ships of the British Royal Navy, and as such, these were carefully regulated. This business alone earned the family a fortune. Wentworth's wide travel, extensive contacts and incorrigible business practices earned him nicknames such as "Don Granada" and "Don Diego" and trained him well for the political life that was to follow.

When the young Wentworth set out in the early 1730s to seek appointment to a seat on the colony's board of trade, Governor Belcher referred to him as a "contemptible simpleton" and "a rascal." But in the ensuing

Benning Wentworth. *New Hampshire Historical Society, Concord, NH.*

political negotiations, it was Wentworth who prevailed, setting the stage for his long, tumultuous and frequently successful career that followed.

In 1741, through maneuverings back in London, New Hampshire was separated from Massachusetts and granted the status of an independent province, with Wentworth as its new governor. He was appointed in large part to appease him after an enormous lumber contract with Spain was canceled. In order for Wentworth to avoid a protracted lawsuit in England, his political friends negotiated with the British government to make him governor of the new colony. His following twenty-five years as governor became the longest such continuous tenure in American colonial history.

For his entire life, Wentworth remained a colorful figure. Reports say that Wentworth was corpulent and crippled by gout and was driven around Portsmouth in a splendid carriage with enough outriders to satisfy a duke. After his wife, Abigail, died, the sixty-four-year-old widower married his beautiful twenty-three-year-old maid Martha Hilton. The marriage created a minor scandal and was immortalized by Henry Wadsworth Longfellow in a poem titled "Lady Wentworth," published in his *Tales of a Wayside Inn*.

Always eager to expand his influence and to profit from his political status, Wentworth was canny in his use of power. Beginning in 1745, the governor extended the dominion of New Hampshire to the west beyond the Connecticut River, taking advantage of the uncertainty of the exact location of the New York border. On January 3, 1749, Governor Wentworth issued a charter for the first new township within the present-day borders of Vermont to be moderated by Colonel William Williams. The six-mile-square territory was to be called Bennington.

In succeeding years, 134 more land grants were issued west of the river, with much of the money going into the pockets of the governor and his family. In 1766 or 1767, Wentworth, one of the wealthiest men in New England, retired and lived in grandeur in Portsmouth until his death in 1770 at the age of seventy-four, without ever having set foot in Vermont.

SAMUEL ROBINSON

1705–1767

The first colonist to see the promise of Bennington was a veteran of the Massachusetts militia during the French and Indian War, Samuel Robinson. It is unclear whether Captain Robinson was born in Cambridge, Massachusetts, in 1705 or 1707. Both dates are frequently cited, but his cenotaph in the Old Bennington Cemetery gives his date of birth as 1705.

For most of his life, Samuel was deeply involved in church and community affairs. His separatist and communitarian views dictated his religious and civic life in Hardwick, Massachusetts, where he was living when he decided to move to the wilderness of Bennington. The issues of freedom of belief and loyalty to a social group guided his leadership of the community.

Around 1756, Captain Robinson passed through the western area of the Hampshire Grants and eastern New York (what is now southwestern Vermont) on his way back home from the war. When the British finally defeated the French after the fall of Montreal and Detroit in 1760, the war was all but over, and Robinson was resolved to settle in the area of today's Bennington. Traveling to Portsmouth, then the capital of New Hampshire, Robinson bought most of the territory comprising Bennington, Pownal, Shaftsbury and Glastenbury. On his return to Hardwick, he encouraged a group of Congregationalist families to purchase land from him and join him in the move to Bennington.

In the spring of 1761, Samuel Robinson, along with his family and followers, arrived in Bennington, prepared for the rigors of pioneer

Samuel Robinson's cenotaph in the Old Bennington Cemetery. *Photograph by Bill Morgan.*

life. Perhaps to be closer to their crops and livestock, most of the settlers decided to build their homes on farmlands rather than in the designated residential center of town. A marker now exists on Monument Avenue in Old Bennington to identify the site of Samuel Robinson's original log cabin. The settlers cleared their land and built homes and barns as quickly as they could. Everything they needed had to be produced locally. The roads the early settlers used were nothing more than Native American paths through the wilderness. The nearest possible support of any size was twenty or forty miles away in the settlements of Williamstown and Albany, respectively.

Robinson reserved the property in Bennington for Congregationalists while directing members of other religious sects, like the Baptists and Episcopalians, to Shaftsbury and Arlington. Within a few months, Bennington had a small but effective town government, with plans for a school and a meetinghouse that would serve as both a church and town hall. By 1762, Robinson and Joseph Safford had established the first saw and gristmills east of town. Although he lived in Bennington for less than six years, Robinson was a key figure in the founding and early development of the area.

The Robinson name reappears frequently in the history of the town founded by the captain. His son General David Robinson, the eighth of his ten surviving children, fought in the Battle of Bennington and was sheriff of the county for twenty-two years. Another son, Moses Robinson, served as the town clerk before he became the governor of Vermont, the state's chief justice and the state's first U.S. senator. Samuel's youngest son, Jonathan Robinson, also became the town clerk, a chief justice of the Vermont Supreme Court and a U.S. senator, and he served in other offices. In 1853, Moses's grandson John S. Robinson was also elected governor of Vermont—the last Democrat to hold that position for one hundred years.

Captain Robinson died of smallpox in 1767 while in London, where he had been sent a year earlier as an emissary in the ongoing dispute between New Hampshire and New York over the land he had purchased and helped settle. The concessions he received at that time provided temporary relief to the settlers. Acting on a report endorsed by Robinson to the Lords of Trade, the king ordered "upon pain of His Majesty's highest displeasure" that no further grants be made in the contested area "until His Majesty's further pleasure should be known." This action provided a much-needed respite from the incursions of the province of New York into the Bennington area. Robinson's body was interred in London, but his grave became a casualty of German bombing during World War II, and its exact location is no longer known.

JEDEDIAH DEWEY

1714–1778

Life in colonial times was deeply grounded in the religious beliefs and policies of the Christian church. One of Bennington's first public buildings, the meetinghouse, also served as its first church, and shortly after the founding of the settlement, those who moved here began looking around for a minister.

Accepting the call was Jedediah Dewey, a native of Westfield, Massachusetts. He was living in Amenia, New York, when the Bennington settlers contacted him in May 1763. They offered him the parcel of land designated as the "minister's right" in the town's charter. That action was confirmed by a vote of support in November that year, following which Reverend Dewey served as the town's pastor until his death fifteen years later.

Dewey joined the Westfield church in 1737 but left it, along with other separatists, in 1749, over the alleged laxity of the "halfway covenant," just one of the many religious controversies of the time. Dewey, a product of the widespread revivalism of the era, was known for his devoutness and strong moral conscience. Though he had only a common-school education and had previously been a carpenter by trade, he soon became the minister of the Westfield Separatists, a splinter group from the established church. In Bennington, he was respected by both progressives and conservatives within the church; a successor described him as being of "catholic and liberal principles."

Dewey's pastorate in Bennington coincided with a period in which the town transformed itself from a tiny, isolated settlement into an important regional center. By the end of his tenure, his congregation had grown to more than 125 members. Although he was loved by his congregation, his pastorate was marked by the strong partisan debates characteristic of that era.

Headstone for Jedediah Dewey's grave, with his name spelled "Jedidiah" here. *Bennington Museum, Bennington, VT.*

As a community leader, Jedediah was active not only in the church itself but also in negotiations with Governor William Tryon of New York during the town's land disputes over the New Hampshire Grants. In 1770, Jedediah was indicted at Albany along with others for being a leader of the hostile settlers' movement aimed at retaining title to their land. In 1772, he was prominently mentioned in the correspondence on the same matter between the New York governor and the citizens of Bennington. Later, he was an advocate of the Patriots' side in the Revolution against the king, as evidenced by a war sermon he gave in August 1777, supporting his congregation's defense of their country. A few days later, his parishioners played an important role at the Battle of Bennington.

Dewey, who was born on April 11, 1714, was married in 1736 to Mindwell Hayden, long before coming to Bennington. He and his wife had eight children, several of whom, including Elijah Dewey, builder of the Walloomsac Inn, and Eldad Dewey, builder of one of the town's early mills, became prominent citizens of Bennington. After the death of Mindwell, which came a few years before Dewey's move to Bennington, Jedediah married Betty Buck and had an additional six children by her. The Dewey family grew to have ties to the Harmons, the Fays and other early settlers of the town. Jedediah died on December 21, 1778, and was buried in the Old Bennington Cemetery near his elaborately carved tombstone, which is engraved with a nontraditional quote from Shakespeare: "Let's talk of graves, and worms, and epitaphs, make dust our paper, and with rainy eyes write sorrow in the bosom of the earth."

STEPHEN FAY AND FAMILY

1715–1781

Like so many of Bennington's early settlers, Stephen Fay was originally a resident of Hardwick, Massachusetts. He became well known in town as the proprietor of the Green Mountain House, later known as the Catamount Tavern. Shortly after he arrived in Bennington in 1766, he built his tavern and became a prominent figure in town and regional affairs. His ten children and their descendants also went on to play key roles in the town's history.

In Fay's time, Bennington was the center of political activity in Vermont, and his tavern, one of the few public buildings in town, became the center of civic activities. Ethan Allen was a friend and neighbor of Fay, and he and his Green Mountain Boys met frequently at the tavern to plan their resistance during the land disputes with New York. The Council of Safety, responsible for citizens' defense in a time of turbulence, met there as well, and several of Fay's children served among its officers. Later, Fay and his wife sent five sons to fight in the Battle of Bennington; the oldest, John, was killed in the conflict.

One anecdote about landlord Fay's attitude at the time of the battle is related as follows:

> *While the families of some of the men engaged in the battle left the vicinity in anticipation of the defeat of our troops, Stephen Fay stood by his tavern. He had received a note from Colonel Baum, the British commander, the day previous, which announced with characteristic coolness and self-confidence,*

> *"My officers and myself will dine with you on the 16th; please have dinner ready." Baum himself fell in the field, but late in the afternoon of the day, many of his officers and men marched through the village under guard as prisoners of war. As they passed the tavern, Mr. Fay stepped out into the porch at the front door, and removing his three-cornered hat with a profound bow, said, "Gentlemen, I am glad to see you, dinner is ready."*

In Bennington, Stephen Fay was known mainly as proprietor of the tavern, but as with many early settlers, his later role in history was played out through his family. Stephen Fay's son Jonas Fay became a versatile and effective civic leader. In 1765, at the age of nineteen, Jonas served as a clerk in the military company of Bennington's first settler, Samuel Robinson, during the French and Indian War. In the years before the Revolution, he also assisted in land negotiations with the governor of New York. Between 1775 and 1777, he drafted documents for important political conventions in Dorset and Westminster. The Westminster Convention resulted in the declaration of Vermont as an independent state, and Jonas Fay is generally considered its author. He was also a practicing physician and, as such, accompanied Ethan Allen on his successful capture of Fort Ticonderoga and served as surgeon to the regiment commanded by Seth Warner during the war. He was later appointed to the state council and the state supreme

The Catamount Tavern in 1869, shortly before it was destroyed by fire. *Bennington Museum, Bennington, VT.*

court. His daughter married the grandson of Reverend Dewey, and his son Heman A. Fay was a graduate of West Point.

Mary, one of Stephen Fay's daughters, became the wife of Vermont Governor Moses Robinson. Another son, Benjamin, took over the tavern after his father's death. He became the first sheriff of the county, and Benjamin's own son Samuel pursued the same calling. Yet another son of Stephen Fay, General Joseph Fay, became the secretary to both the Council of Safety and the state council and served for three years as Vermont's secretary of state. Joseph's grandson the Honorable Theodore Sedgwick Fay later became United States' minister to Switzerland as well as a popular author.

Stephen Fay, the patriarch of the family, passed on to his progeny a lasting legacy of dedicated civic responsibility. When told of his eldest son, John's, death at the Battle of Bennington, Stephen asked only if John had behaved bravely. Assured by witnesses that he had, Stephen is said to have replied: "Then I am satisfied." He then prepared his son's body for burial himself.

Fay's famous and historic Catamount Tavern was lost to fire in 1871. The Bennington Museum owns his old tavern ledger that shows Ethan Allen's dinner account. Today, a monument complete with a statue of a catamount marks the spot near where the tavern stood on Monument Avenue.

MARGARET BOWEN

CIRCA 1742–UNKNOWN

A Black woman named Margaret Bowen (called Pegg) was enslaved by Captain Stephen Fay in Bennington from 1772 to 1778. Slavery was not uncommon in the northern colonies, and there are several examples of early white settlers bringing enslaved people with them to Bennington. The Black population in eighteenth-century Vermont is hard to calculate. When the first federal census was taken in 1791, after Vermont joined the Union, there were 20 Black people counted in Bennington out of a population of 2,350, but not all of these people were enslaved.

Pegg was born around 1742. She was enslaved by Moses Porter of Hadley, Massachusetts, in 1754, after he constructed a grand new house on a property he called "Forty Acres." When Porter died in 1756, his estate inventory listed two enslaved people, Pegg Bowen and Zebulon Prutt, who were then inherited by Porter's daughter and son-in-law, Elizabeth and Charles Phelps Jr. Pegg had two daughters, Rose, born on July 2, 1761, and Phillis, born on June 2, 1765.

In May 1771, Pegg and an enslaved man named Pompe Morgan requested that the town clerk in Hadley record their intent to marry. They needed the consent of both of their enslavers, which Pompe's enslaver, Jon Warner, refused to give. Pegg seemed to have had more agency. In August 1771, she "went out for herself," an arrangement in which she worked for another family, but her enslavers collected her wages. She may have been allowed to keep a portion of the money, or she might have sought this

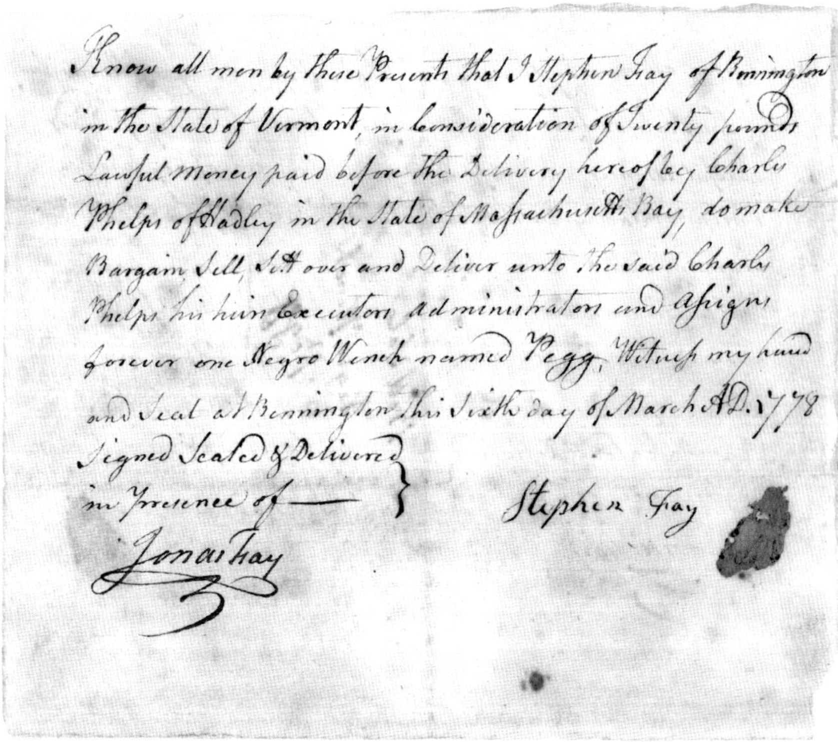

Know all men by these Presents that I Stephen Fay of Bennington in the State of Vermont, in Consideration of Twenty pounds Lawful Money paid before the Delivery hereof by Charles Phelps of Hadley in the State of Massachusetts Bay do make Bargain Sell Sett over and Deliver unto the said Charles Phelps his heirs Executors Administrators and Assigns forever one Negro Wench named Pegg. Witness my hand and Seal at Bennington this Sixth day of March AD. 1778

Signed Sealed & Delivered in Presence of — Jonas Fay

Stephen Fay

Receipt for the sale of the enslaved Pegg Bowen by Stephen Fay to Charles Phelps in 1778. *Porter-Phelps-Huntington Family Papers, Robert S. Cox Special Collections and University Archives Research Center, UMass Amherst Libraries.*

arrangement simply to be nearer her intended spouse. Nearly a year later, a solution presented itself. Stephen Fay, in Bennington, would purchase both Pegg and Pompe together; presumably, Pompe's enslaver gave in. At this point, it appears Pegg was given a choice. She could go to Vermont with her lover or stay in Massachusetts with her children (Rose and Phillis were eleven and seven years old, respectively). She chose her husband.

We know very little about Pegg's life in Bennington. Back in Hadley, her daughter Rose gave birth to a child on April 18, 1775. Three days later, Pegg's other daughter, Phillis, died of tuberculosis, and the new baby was named after her. Pegg did not meet her granddaughter until she was sold back to Charles Phelps Jr. on March 6, 1778, for twenty pounds. We do not know what happened to Pegg's husband, Pompe. He may have died in Bennington or been sold to another enslaver, or perhaps he gained his freedom.

There was a great deal of ambivalence regarding slavery in early Vermont. The Vermont Constitution, signed on July 8, 1777, declared an end to the enslavement of adults, but it had vague language and came without any provision for enforcement. The first article of chapter 1 stated:

> *That all men are born equally free and independent.... Therefore, no male person, born in this country, or brought from over sea, ought to be holden by law, to serve any person, as a servant, slave or apprentice, after he arrives to the age of twenty-one years, nor female, in like manner, after she arrives to the age of eighteen years, unless they are bound by their own consent, after they arrive to such age, or bound by law, for the payment of debts, damages, fines, costs, or the like.*

The constitution's use of weak wording (*ought* instead of *shall*) might have been intentional.

Stephen Fay's son Jonas was the witness of Fay's 1778 sale of Pegg. Jonas Fay was a delegate to the 1777 constitutional convention in Windsor and is generally credited as the constitution's primary author. Just because the constitution was signed did not mean that everyone abided by it. There was no ratification process, many people opposed the new government and a difficulty in printing even delayed the first elections. People like the Fays clearly did not think the prohibition of the enslavement of adults was binding. On October 24, 1778, the Vermont legislature appointed a committee to prepare a bill regarding the freedom of enslaved people, but no bill was ever presented, and no record exists of their actions.

Both Stephen and Jonas Fay had to be aware of the fact that enslaving people was against the spirit of the new constitution, if not the letter of the law. Presumably, Pegg herself was either not aware of this or was not in a position to do anything about it. Pegg's value at twenty pounds was far less than her appraised value of thirty-three pounds and some change in 1756, and it is possible that Fay chose to sell her at a loss rather than acknowledge the freedom that was rightfully hers. It is also possible that her value to her enslavers had fallen due to her age and the end of her prime childbearing years.

Fay did have contemporaries who were very much opposed to slavery and actually acted on their beliefs. After Ebenezer Allen captured a Black woman and her young daughter, who had been enslaved in Burgoyne's army, he freed them. He did not cite the Vermont Constitution in his manumission notice, recorded in Bennington by the town clerk on

November 27, 1777, but stated, "It is not right in the sight of God to keep slaves." Other Vermonters may have felt the same way, but most, like Jonas Fay, were silent witnesses.

A year after Pegg returned to Hadley, her daughter Rose became sick. She continued to battle what appears to have been tuberculosis until her death on March 14, 1781. She was only twenty years old. Her daughter, Phillis (Pegg's granddaughter), also suffered from tuberculosis and died two years later.

Pegg finally gained her freedom in May 1782. Whether the Phelps family had formally manumitted her or she purchased her freedom is, again, unclear. There were several court cases taking place in Massachusetts at this time that ended up making slavery untenable in the state.

SLAVERY AND AFRICAN AMERICANS IN BENNINGTON

One would think that slavery was not an issue in Bennington, since Vermont was the first state to outlaw the practice in its constitution on July 2, 1777. In fact, there were several other enslaved people in Bennington in addition to Pegg Bowen, and they deserve mention here. The number of enslaved people in Vermont in 1770 was estimated to be about twenty-five, most of them living in Bennington, but when the state's constitution was passed, they weren't all instantly emancipated. The letter of the law was that existing enslaved men at that time had to wait until they were twenty-one years of age to be freed, and women had to wait until they were eighteen. By the time of the 1790 census, there were still sixteen or seventeen enslaved people in the state, all of them in Bennington; however, there is some controversy about whether this was a correct figure due to the odd way the tally was kept. Unfortunately, very little is known about any of these enslaved people—such was the nature of slavery.

One of the more unexpected cases seems to be that of Reverend David Avery (1746–1818), who was installed as the second pastor of the Congregational church following Jedediah Dewey's tenure. Avery left the Bennington church in 1783 after preaching here only three years. He received strong criticism from the community for bringing a Black woman with him as an enslaved laborer. Her name is unrecorded, but she was bound in service to Avery while he lived on West Street in a house that once stood on the foundation of today's Four Chimney's Inn. It wasn't a case without controversy; in fact, one of his parishioners was excommunicated for refusing to acknowledge the pastor's right to own an enslaved person. Avery also held certain religious beliefs that weren't shared by his congregation, which further hastened his departure.

Even Ethan Allen's family is known to have held enslaved people. His brother enslaved people and so did Allen's daughter, Lucy Caroline Hitchcock. In fact, his daughter brought two people, a mother and child, with her from Alabama in 1835 and kept them in Vermont for at least six years before the woman's husband was able to buy her freedom from Lucy. It is believed by some historians that Ethan himself enslaved people.

Another Black man, Nimrod Greenleaf (1780–circa 1865), lived in Bennington with his wife, Margaret Smith Greenleaf (circa 1791–1858), and was buried in the Village Cemetery on Morgan Street. In 1846, an article appeared in the newspaper apparently for the purpose of keeping slave catchers from seizing Nimrod and taking him south. It read:

> *We the undersigned hereby certify that for ten or twelve years past, Nimrod Greenleaf has been an inhabitant of the town of Bennington, and that during the above time we have been personally acquainted with said Greenleaf, that he has at all times sustained a good character for honesty, industry and sobriety, and we most cheerfully state that during the time of our acquaintance with him we have never heard the least report calculated to impair his moral character.*

The Greenleafs were probably formerly enslaved people from Connecticut who came to Vermont in 1810 and raised their family here.

Charles "Pompey" Vanderburg (1790–1883) was born into slavery in Kinderhook, New York. In 1803, he was taken from his parents and forced to work in Troy and then Hoosick. In 1816, he managed to escape from the Hoosick farm and crossed the state line into Vermont, hoping to avoid being traded for a horse and taken back to Troy. He was able to remain a free man in Vermont for the rest of his life, and he worked as a laborer and raised a family with his wife, Lorinda. The family lived near Beech Street and Gore Road, east of town. Although there is no gravestone, it is believed that Pompey might be buried with his family in the Village Cemetery.

When Vermont joined the United States in 1791, it was (on paper) a free state. The first Vermont state census reported only free Black people living in the state. The *Vermont Gazette*, published in Bennington by Anthony Haswell, in its issue from September 26, 1791, stated, "The return of the marshal's assistant for the county of Bennington shows that there are in the county…17 black males over 4 and under 16; 15 black females. Total of inhabitants 12,254. To the honor of humanity, no slaves."

The *Gazette*'s assertion was naive and optimistic. There were indeed examples of enslaved Vermonters up through the 1840s at least, and to our shame, slavery's legacy of racism still haunts us.

Some local documents and newspaper articles give hints about the presence of other enslaved people, too. For instance, the 1782 will of a local farmer named John Armstrong lists a "negro boy valued at 60 pounds" among his possessions.

An interesting footnote to the history of slavery is that until recently, the age exemption for slavery was still on the books in Vermont. By Vermont law, you could technically still enslave a person who was under twenty-one years of age until the voters of the state passed an amendment to the constitution in 2022. Sadly, the vote was only 81 percent in favor of abolition. The rest of the voters felt that the loophole should remain on the books.

JAMES BREAKENRIDGE

1721–1783

On August 15, 1927, a bronze marker was unveiled along Murphy Road to declare that the state of Vermont was born there. Although a bit hyperbolic, the fact remains that if the events that took place near this monument in 1771 hadn't happened, there might not have been a state of Vermont. This marks the site of the homestead of James Breakenridge (sometimes spelled "Breckenridge" or even "Brakenridge") in the early days of settlement and a focal point of the territory's land dispute with New York.

Breakenridge was born in Ireland on May 28, 1721. His parents brought him to America when he was six years old and settled in Palmer Center, Massachusetts, a small town halfway between Springfield and Sturbridge. As a young man, he married Mary Moore of Ware, Massachusetts, in 1745 with whom he had at least a dozen children, half of them born in Ware and half of them born after they moved to Bennington. They arrived here in the fall of 1761, following his service in the French and Indian War. Breakenridge's arrival with about twenty families was immediately on the heels of the first wave of settlers who had been led by Samuel Robinson. As one of the town's wealthiest landowners, Breakenridge was elected a selectman at the first town meeting in early 1762.

James purchased his property under the New Hampshire Grants, but it wasn't long before landowners in New York claimed his property as their own, saying that all the land west of the Connecticut River was rightfully theirs. On December 28, 1763, Lieutenant Governor Cadwallader Colden of New York issued a proclamation in support of the New Yorkers' claims despite New Hampshire Governor Wentworth's sales to the settlers. This precipitated a heated dispute over who really owned the property. Since the Bennington pioneers had already started building homes and improving their lands, it wasn't an easy thing to just up and leave, so they banded together and decided to fight. Two farmers, James Breakenridge and Dr. Josiah Fuller, were singled out by the New York officials as test cases to challenge the validity of their claims. On October 19, 1769, the New Yorkers' surveyors arrived to do their work and were chased off by the local residents.

Since the case was to be tried and adjudicated in an Albany court, the settlers felt that they would certainly lose, so at a meeting in the Catamount Tavern, they decided to form a militant group that came to be called the Green Mountain Boys to physically prevent a New York takeover. Breakenridge hired Ethan Allen to represent his claim in court, and as expected, in June 1770, the courts ruled against the settlers. When the judge advised Allen to go home and convince the settlers to either abandon their farms or rent them from the New York claimants, Ethan forcefully replied that he would not, using his famous words as a warning: "The Gods of the valleys are not the Gods of the hills."

On July 18, 1771, Albany Sheriff Hendrick Ten Eyck marched from Albany with a posse of 150 men to survey the land and evict Breakenridge, but the next morning, they were met near the present-day Henry Bridge by a group of local men. They refused to let them pass but agreed to let the sheriff and a small number of his men go to Breakenridge's house to talk the matter over. The Bennington Mob, an armed group of about 250 men, was stationed nearby in Breakenridge's fields, so upon seeing them, the sheriff decided to avoid a confrontation and returned to Albany. This incident became known as the Breakenridge Standoff.

Although no shots were fired that day, a warrant was issued for the arrest of Breakenridge, and a reward was offered. As Hiland Hall wrote, "Here in fact, on the farm of James Brackenridge was born the future state of Vermont." In 1772, James Breakenridge and Jehiel Hawley of Arlington were chosen to travel to London to plead their case before King George III. Hawley decided against making the trip, but Breakenridge went on alone, hoping to get the king to recognize the settlers' claims. Breakenridge was too mild-mannered for the job, and his arguments went unheard, but before long, the start of the American Revolution made it a moot issue. No one cared what the king thought after that, and Breakenridge, along with Heman Allen and Jonas Fay, had to represent the New Hampshire grantees again, this time before the newly formed Continental Congress.

Breakenridge died on April 16, 1783, at the age of sixty-two, just before the Treaty of Paris was signed in September, ending the war. At the time of Breakenridge's death, his estate was valued at £4,841 and included 846 acres of land, herds of sheep and cattle, a gristmill and a sawmill. The Breakenridge house stood until 1889 when it, like so many of Bennington's old wooden buildings, was destroyed by fire.

JOHN STARK

1728–1822

New Hampshire's General John Stark is the acknowledged hero of the Battle of Bennington. His oft-quoted remarks, "The redcoats are ours, or Molly Stark sleeps a widow tonight," represents only one facet of this New England soldier. He contributed mightily, by both his commanding presence and his actual role in the battle, to one of the key colonial victories of the American Revolution.

Although Stark had enjoyed extensive military experience, on the eve of the battle, he was a private citizen. A decade earlier, he served with the British as a second lieutenant with Rogers' Rangers in the French and Indian War. Later, against the British at Bunker Hill, he was said to be responsible for holding the line in that key battle. Then in 1776, he fought under George Washington at the Battles of Trenton and Princeton but saw lesser officers promoted before him. The prickly Stark retired from military service as a result and returned home to New Hampshire. Pressed by necessity, New Hampshire asked Stark to consider a new appointment as brigadier general. With the proviso that he be allowed to act under the authority of the state alone, independent of the Continental army, Stark accepted.

The resources Stark brought to the battle turned out to be invaluable. He was a favorite among the troops, and his military experience, which gave him the ability to gain and interpret intelligence, proved crucial. It was Stark who first learned that British General John Burgoyne was preparing to dispatch

John Stark. *Bennington Museum, Bennington, VT.*

a force to march to Bennington to capture supplies and munitions stored here. Stark immediately set off for the town, arriving a week ahead of the enemy.

After five days spent in reconnaissance and consultation with authorities at Bennington, Stark was well prepared for the action to come. Though outnumbered, Stark combined his skill as a military strategist with fortuitous timing on the day of the battle. He summoned Seth Warner's troops, who were waiting in reserve, and their arrival, just in the nick of time, allowed the colonists to prevail in a much-needed victory. The British defeat at Bennington deprived Burgoyne of supplies, and he lost approximately 20 percent of his forces. It set the stage for the much larger British defeat at Saratoga two months later, which is considered by most historians to be the turning point of the Revolution.

A sense of the precariousness of the situation facing the colonists and their determination to prevail is evident in a letter sent out from Bennington to its neighbors by the Council of Safety on the day before the battle: "August 15, 1777. Sir: You are hereby desired to forward to this place, by express, all the lead you can possibly collect in your vicinity, as it is expected every minute an action will commence between our troops and the enemy within four or five miles of this place, and the lead will be positively wanted."

Later in his life, Stark was recognized for the extraordinary expertise he brought to his military endeavors. Not only had he played key roles at both Bunker Hill and Bennington, but in the view of historians, his bravery and ability to think under fire had also produced a career unblemished by a single notable military failure. Although he was little educated and somewhat brusque, he nonetheless garnered near-universal approbation. Even as late as 1805, then-President Thomas Jefferson wrote the general a personal letter of praise.

Interestingly, Stark's most famous statement was penned in a letter to fellow veterans of the Battle of Bennington on the occasion of a reunion of soldiers in 1809. Along with stating his regret that he could not attend due to old age, the general appended a suggested toast for those gathered: "Live free or die: Death is not the worst of evils." In 1822, Stark died at the age of ninety-four, the oldest surviving general of the Revolution. His wife, Molly, canonized in his call to battle, had died some eight years before. In 1945, his phrase "Live Free or Die" was adopted as the official state motto of his native New Hampshire.

ETHAN ALLEN

1738–1789

In the early days, Bennington's most famous resident was Ethan Allen, who came to the fledgling town in 1766, about five years after its founding. Allen and his family, who all arrived in the area at about the same time, hailed from Connecticut, having heard of the new settlement from neighbors and friends. Among the Allen relatives who played a role in Bennington at the time of the Revolution were Allen's cousins Ebenezer Allen, Remember Baker and Seth Warner, all active in the hostilities with Britain and New York, and his brother Ira Allen. Ira became a key player along with Ethan in the political and economic development of the state. In addition, Ira was the author of one of the state's first published histories, *The Natural and Political History of the State of Vermont*, in 1798.

As the eldest of a large family, Ethan Allen assumed the responsibility for his mother and siblings following his father's death in 1755. After a brief stint in the military, he led a varied career in farming and business in both Cornwall and Salisbury, Connecticut. He also engaged in the profitable speculation of land. Early on, he displayed a strong intellect and had spiritual interests, but the demands of providing for his family kept him from attending college as he had intended. Allen was already known for his talents as an advocate by the time he came to Bennington, and he made good use of his writing abilities to champion causes he believed in strongly. He was a tall and imposing figure, and people described him as strong-willed, energetic, inventive and impulsive.

Ethan Allen. *Author's collection.*

Along with his brothers, Ethan speculated heavily in the disputed lands called the New Hampshire Grants. Due to these real estate investments, it was crucial that the government recognize their claims to the land. Allen therefore found himself pressed into service in the quarrels between Bennington and other New Hampshire Grant communities against the government of New York. Shortly after he arrived in Bennington, Ethan began to negotiate in Albany for the rights to the land sold to them by New Hampshire's Governor Wentworth. In the early 1770s, attempts by New York officials to forcibly roust settlers like James Breakenridge from their farms around Bennington led to the formation of the Green Mountain Boys. This organization, led by Ethan Allen and his extended family, succeeded in turning back the New Yorkers through a program of coercion and intimidation intended to discourage the "Yorkers" from pursuing their own claims to the land. The Allens and their compatriots proved extremely effective at this.

However, these internal colonial land disputes were disrupted by the outbreak of war with Britain. After the battles of Lexington and Concord in April 1775, in which Massachusetts minutemen faced red-coated regulars of the British army and fired "the shot heard 'round the world," Allen responded to entreaties from his friends to take action. In May that year, Ethan assembled the Green Mountain Boys and preemptively seized the British fortifications at Ticonderoga and Crown Point without any loss of life. Plans for this mission, the first offensive action against the British of the American Revolution, were formulated by Allen and his officers in the council room at the Catamount Tavern in Bennington.

While Allen was successful in these and other early exploits, his penchant for action led him to initiate an independent attack on the British in Canada later that same summer. This proved to be a disaster, and Allen was captured and spent several years in prison in England, causing him to miss the bulk of the war. Finally, in 1778, he was released in a prisoner exchange.

After the war, the publication of Allen's philosophical tract *Reason: The Only Oracle of Man* in 1785 marked Ethan's move into other controversial areas. It was printed in Bennington by Anthony Haswell and paid for by the liquidation of some of the land Allen and his family had been steadily acquiring over the years. In 1787, Allen moved his family to a large farm located near present-day Burlington, which became his home for the rest of his life. He remained active until the end, involving himself in causes, such as an ownership dispute between settlers and the government of Pennsylvania, as well as the political and economic struggles of Vermont, which led to the state's financial stability and its ultimate acceptance as the nation's fourteenth state.

Unfortunately, Allen didn't live to see Vermont's statehood himself. He died near his farm on February 12, 1789, at the age of fifty-one, a recognized hero of the nation and the region. An iconoclast to the end, he requested that his funeral service be private and exclude all ministers, sermons and public prayers.

MOSES ROBINSON

1741–1813

On March 22, 1741, Moses Robinson was born in Hardwick, part of Worcester County, Massachusetts. He was the sixth son of the large Robinson family of Samuel and Mercy Robinson and became one of the most prominent of their children. He went to study at Dartmouth College in the years before his father led a group of settlers to Bennington at the end of the French and Indian War. At the age of twenty, he joined up with them to help clear the land and build homes here. From 1762 until 1781, Moses served as the town clerk, and like his father, he farmed and speculated in land. After serving on the Council of Safety for several years, he joined the Vermont militia as a colonel and fought during the Revolution. He led his regiment in the evacuation of Mount Independence following the British army's recovery of Fort Ticonderoga.

Moses married Mary Fay, the daughter of Stephen Fay, who owned the Catamount Tavern and was a leader of the Green Mountain Boys. Mary died at an early age after giving birth to six children. Moses then married Susannah Warner, the daughter of General Jonathan Warner, but did not have any children with her. Even though Moses had no formal legal training, he had a talent for leadership and became the first chief justice of the new Republic of Vermont. On October 13, 1789, Moses Robinson became the republic's second governor. Vermont didn't become a state until 1791, and Moses was active in the negotiations that led to its admission to the Union. At that time, he became the first U.S. senator from Vermont, but he resigned from the office in 1796 after serving five years of his six-year term. As a strong supporter of an anti-administration faction, he sided with the new

Artist's interpretation of the 1791 meeting in Bennington between Moses Robinson, Thomas Jefferson, James Madison, Isaac Tichenor and Elijah Dewey. *Bennington Museum, Bennington, VT.*

Democratic-Republican Party of Thomas Jefferson and wanted nothing to do with the administration of John Adams. After his resignation, the only other public office he held was in the Vermont House of Representatives, where he served for a single term in 1802.

Moses Robinson famously hosted his friends then–Secretary of State Thomas Jefferson and Virginia Congressman James Madison at his house in Bennington in 1791. They came to visit Vermont for three days on what they called their "Northern Journey." It was a combination vacation and fact-finding trip in which they hoped to see Americans in their natural element. Jefferson seemed to soak up new ideas wherever he went, and Bennington was no exception. Here, he saw the possibility of turning the local maple sugar industry into something that would eliminate the entire country's need for imported sugar. The pair arrived in town on Saturday, planning to move on the next day, but since it was Sunday and Vermont's strict laws prohibited travel on Sunday, Robinson took them to the Congregational meetinghouse for worship. Jefferson and Madison shocked the local congregation by telling Parson Swift that they hadn't been to a church service in years.

Following his death on May 26, 1813, Moses Robinson was buried with other members of his family in Bennington's Old Cemetery on the hill.

SETH WARNER

1743–1784

One of Bennington's most successful military leaders of the late eighteenth century was Seth Warner. He lived a short life and died at the age of forty-one, but in those few years, he played an instrumental role in shaping the future of Bennington, Vermont, and the nation. Warner was born on May 17, 1743, in Roxbury, Connecticut, which, at the time, was called Woodbury. His father and grandfather were both medical doctors, and the family probably believed Seth would become a country doctor as well. Although Seth knew a good deal about medicine from their example, his experiences in the militia as a teenager during the French and Indian War whetted his appetite for a military life. When Seth was twenty, his father purchased land in the New Hampshire Grants in the part of Bennington then known as Riverside, now sometimes called Irish Corners. Their acreage was located around today's Henry Bridge, and a monument has been placed near the site of Warner's house just off Murphy Road. Like so many of the town's older wooden structures, it burned in 1858. After that 1763 purchase, the family probably spent the first few summers clearing the fields and planting crops. In the winters, they returned to Connecticut until they moved permanently to Bennington in 1765. Seth's house must have been similar to the Henry House, which still stands nearby and whose frame was raised on the same day as Seth's in 1769.

In 1927, the *Bennington Banner* waxed poetic about Warner when it said:

> *Seth Warner was a handsome young man. It is said that when he rode at the head of his Green Mountain Boys armed and equipped for duty, no one*

Seth Warner monument. *Photograph by Bill Morgan.*

> *could have carried himself with more grace and dignity. With a broad and intellectual forehead relieved by a profusion of nut-brown hair, and with sparkling blue eyes beaming forth under eyebrows most beautifully arched, his physiognomy gave unmistakable signs of an intelligent courageous and energetic man.*

By the late 1760s, the land disputes between the area's settlers and New York State landowners were well underway. Young Warner was elected a captain in the town's militia and was there to lead the local farmers in the showdown known as the Breakenridge Standoff. He, along with Ethan Allen and Warner's cousin Remember Baker, were the leaders of the group known as the Green Mountain Boys. When the Albany sheriff came to forcibly evict Breakenridge from his farm, Warner assembled his men, and the sheriff withdrew without bloodshed. A reward was offered for Warner and some of the other ringleaders, but he was never captured, and his case was never pursued.

As the American Revolution engulfed western New England, Warner was promoted to full colonel through his leadership in the capture of Crown Point followed by the Battle of Longueuil, the Siege of Quebec and the Battle of Hubbardton. These all led up to the pivotal battle of Bennington on August 16, 1777. In the summer of 1777, British General John Burgoyne led his forces south from Canada. Their strategy was to invade as far south as Albany, where they would join up with other British forces coming from the west and south and thereby cut the colonies in half. One thing Burgoyne hadn't planned well was his supply chain, and he found that the farther away from Canada he went, the scarcer the supplies that any army needed for survival. To remedy this, General Burgoyne sent a large portion of his troops under Colonel Friedrich Baum toward Bennington to seize the storehouse that had been set up for the Continental army.

Warner, whose farmland was right in the path of Baum's army, knew the area well and was therefore very helpful in planning the defense of Bennington. His own troops had just been pushed back to Manchester after the Battle of Hubbardton, and they were awaiting orders while Warner met with General John Stark to plan a counterattack on the British. Warner summoned his troops to march as quickly as possible the twenty-five miles to the battlefield, where Stark's men had beaten back Baum's forces through the day's fighting. Just as British reinforcements sent by Burgoyne got to the battlefield, Warner's militia arrived and routed the British. It was an unmistakable victory for the Patriots and one that helped turn the tide of the war, resulting in Burgoyne's surrender at Saratoga a month later and the eventual defeat of the British.

Stark and Warner deployed their forces to Saratoga and were able to keep Burgoyne's troops from escaping. For the rest of the war, Seth Warner played an important role, but nothing surpassed his victory at Bennington. After the war, Warner was made a brigadier general, the only person to attain that rank from the new independent state of Vermont.

Warner's health had never been good, but in 1780, he was seriously wounded in an attack by Native Americans near Fort George, and he retired from active service and went home. For most of his adult life, he had been away from his family and his farm due to his military service. Now, he stayed in his house in Bennington for nearly two years until 1781, when, in failing health, he moved back to Roxbury, where he died on December 26, 1784. By then, he was penniless, and his property had to be sold by his widow to pay his debts. A century later, the Town of Roxbury erected a tall obelisk over Warner's grave, and in 1911, a statue of Warner was erected by the Bennington Historical Society on the grounds of the battle monument.

LEMUEL HAYNES

1753–1833

One remarkable man who visited Bennington several times in the early days was often called the "Black Puritan." His real name was Lemuel Haynes, and for years, he was the pastor in nearby Rutland and Manchester. On several occasions, he was invited to speak from the pulpit of the Old First Church and is depicted preaching in a large painting that now hangs in the galleries of the Bennington Museum.

Lemuel Haynes led an incredible life for his time. He was born illegitimate to a white mother and a Black father in West Hartford, Connecticut, on July 18, 1753. The Haynes name was not from his father or mother but came from the family who took in his mother at the time of Lemuel's birth. When Lemuel was just five months old, he was indentured to a farmer named David Rose in Granville, Massachusetts. As a bond servant, he was pledged to remain with the Rose family until he was twenty-one. However, the Rose family was charitable, and they raised Lemuel as one of their own children. They sent him to the village school, and being devout Christians, they often asked him to read from the Bible and other religious works.

In 1775, Lemuel left the farm behind. He served briefly as a minuteman after the skirmishes of Lexington and Concord and then volunteered as a member of the militia that was sent to relieve the colonists after Ethan Allen's seizure of Fort Ticonderoga. It was in that year that he made his first visit to Bennington while marching north with the troops. They stopped to attend a Sunday service offered by Reverend Jedediah Dewey in the old meetinghouse. Fifty years later, Haynes came back to preach from the pulpit of the new church and quoted from Dewey's original text. Following his

Lemuel Haynes. *Bennington Museum, Bennington, VT.*

service in the Continental army, Lemuel began to formally study for the ministry with Reverend Daniel Farrand in Canaan, Connecticut. He was ordained on November 9, 1785, the first Black man to be accepted as a leader in the church. In spite of his eloquence as a speaker, Haynes was not given a church in Connecticut because of the color of his skin. Undaunted by this refusal, he moved to Vermont, where the congregations were somewhat less prejudiced, and he worked as an itinerant missionary, riding his horse from town to town preaching the gospel. He married a white schoolteacher named Elizabeth Babbitt in 1783 before his permanent move to Vermont, and he had nine or ten children with her.

In 1788, Reverend Haynes was invited to become the pastor at West Rutland, where he remained for almost thirty years. During his tenure there, his congregation grew from forty-two members to over three hundred. He became very popular as a speaker and was invited to many churches in the southwestern corner of Vermont, including several visits to Bennington. His sermons were so well received that many of them were published, and his fame spread throughout New England. He was given an honorary degree from Middlebury College in 1804, an honor reserved for only the greatest theologians at the time. In 1817, he was dismissed from the West Rutland church and moved to Manchester, Vermont, where he lived for four years before he moved on to Granville, New York, where he preached until his death in 1833.

The Bennington Museum's painting of Haynes is by the artist William Tefft Schwarz. It was unveiled by John Spargo in 1939, more than one hundred years after Haynes's death. It depicts Reverend Haynes giving a sermon at the Old First Church in Bennington and was painted with great attention to detail. Many of the faces of the parishioners were modeled after old paintings and daguerreotypes of the people who might have been there to hear Haynes preach. Newspapers on July 5, 1820, described a similar occasion, when they said, "He [Lemuel] seemed to have caught the spirit of his vocation; his manner was fervent, as if under the special out-pourings of faith and charity, and by Divine instruction."

DAVID REDDING

CIRCA 1754–1778

In 1976, the skeleton of a man who had died two hundred years earlier was finally laid to rest in the Old Bennington Cemetery. The bones belonged to David Redding, a man accused and found guilty of acting as a Tory spy during the Revolutionary War. He was hanged in Bennington on June 11, 1778, for what his accusers called "inimical conduct." As a result of his treason, he was denied a decent burial, and his skeleton was used to teach anatomy at Williams College. His early loyalty to King George III of England still made his interment here controversial in the twentieth century, and his burial took place with little ceremony or public notice.

The facts about David Redding are still largely unknown; in fact, we know much more about Redding's final week than we know about the rest of his life. Many of the details of his crime and trial have been lost to history. John Spargo, the first director of the Bennington Museum, wrote an entire book about Redding in 1945 called *The Story of David Redding Who Was Hanged*, in which Spargo tried somewhat unsuccessfully to uncover the facts of his biography.

Redding, whose name might have also been spelled "Reddin," "Riddeng" or even "Reading," may have been born in New York State sometime in 1754. Around the time of the Battle of Bennington, his family may have been living around Hoosick, and Redding himself may have taken part in the battle with the local Loyalists on the side of the British. He seems to have been a member of Colonel John Peters's Queen's Loyal Rangers regiment at one time, but whether he was still actively in the military at the time of

David Redding's grave in the Old Bennington Cemetery. *Photograph by Bill Morgan.*

his arrest is unknown. If he was, he would have been entitled to a military trial and court-martial, although the outcome and sentence would probably have been the same in either case. In 1778, he was arrested, only to escape while en route to Albany for trial. He was captured again in Bennington and accused of stealing either horses or guns from the home of David Robinson with the intention of giving them to the enemy. He escaped at least once more from Fay's Tavern, where he was being held, and then recaptured near Hoosick, New York.

The trial records of his June 4, 1778 court appearance might have been burned in the 1809 fire that destroyed Bennington's first courthouse or purposely misplaced, but one way or another, the trial transcript does not seem to exist. It is known that Colonel Samuel Robinson Jr. and Jeremiah Clark acted as judges and presided over the trial, even though it was not within their jurisdiction. John Burnham, a local man who knew something about legal matters, might have represented Redding after the six jurors found him guilty. Treason was a crime punishable by death, and Redding was sentenced to be hanged. When it was pointed out to Governor Thomas Chittenden that under English law, a prisoner was entitled to be tried by a jury of twelve men, a second trial was quickly scheduled for June 9, with Ethan Allen acting as the state's attorney. The crowd was so eager to see Redding hanged that Allen dramatically promised them that if the accused wasn't hanged on June 11, as scheduled, they could hang him instead. It was a needless promise. The appointed jury of twelve did find Redding guilty a few days later, and a "vast multitude" gathered on June 11 to witness the execution.

The proceedings are shrouded in mystery, since the facts surrounding the case seem vague and the original arrests were made in New York and not in the new Republic of Vermont. Some have suggested that the court records went missing in order to cover up the inadequacies of the trial itself.

After Redding's body was cut down by Sheriff Benjamin Fay, the body was taken away by Dr. Jonas Fay, who decided to preserve the skeleton, since no one wanted to claim a traitor's body. By 1927, Redding's bones had found their way to the Bennington Museum, where they were kept in a box. Forty-six years later, they were finally buried in the cemetery below a marker that simply identified him as "David Redding Loyalist Executed 1778."

JOSEPH HAVILAND

1718–UNKNOWN

The settlement of what became North Bennington began in 1761, when Joseph Haviland, a Quaker, arrived and built a log cabin near the present intersection of West and Church Streets. Somewhat later, around 1777, Haviland and his son-in-law, Moses Sage, built the first gristmill on the water privilege that later became the site of the Stark Paper Mill, now repurposed as a group of attractive townhouses called Haviland's Privilege. The millstones from the original gristmill have been cut in half and are now used as the lintels for the windows on the newer building.

Haviland held title to the land under grants from both New York and New Hampshire. Water rights to the stream were called "privileges," and Joseph's privilege included most of what is now Paran Creek. At first, both the place (Haviland Mills) and stream (Haviland Brook) were known by Haviland's name. In 1776 or 1777, Haviland was denounced as a Tory, and his property was seized by the local Council of Safety. His son-in-law, Sage, was a well-known Patriot and was successful in his bid to take over the mill and real estate. Thereafter, the town became Sage's City. According to a much later report in the *Bennington Banner*, "In June 1778, the General Assembly, sitting in this town, after full investigation, found that William Haviland, Moses Sage and James Rogers, were the real owners and [the property] was restored to them."

After Haviland was put in prison in New York State in the summer of 1777 for conspiring with fellow Loyalist Philip Skene to gather ammunition to use against the Patriots, the name of the stream was changed to Paran Creek, possibly a reference to a wilderness area in the Bible. Haviland's daughter married Patriot Sage, but due to the political strife, Haviland is said to have disowned her and left the area, never to return.

MOSES SAGE

1754–1816

Among the earliest followers of Joseph Haviland, who came to settle within the limits of today's North Bennington, was Captain Moses Sage. After Haviland left in 1777, Sage became the area's most prominent citizen for the next forty years. He arrived in the village in 1776 on the eve of the Revolution and went into business with his father-in-law, Joseph Haviland, after marrying his daughter Susannah Ann Haviland that same year. Sage was a Patriot and opposed to his father-in-law's allegiance to the king. After Haviland left town, Moses became the village's leading businessman. He was so important that in 1776, the town was renamed Sage's City and remained so until 1828, when it was officially renamed North Bennington. Sage's commercial interests grew to include mills, general stores, real estate and blast furnaces. Despite Vermont's early abolition of slavery, it appears that Moses might have enslaved at least one person. In the 1800 census, one Black person is listed as living in the Sage household. Although the census lists the person as "free," a memoir written by Almira D. Stewart assures us that the person was indeed enslaved. The evidence is contradictory, but in the early years of Vermont, there were people who were known to enslave people.

North Bennington's abundant waterpower, provided by both Paran Creek and the Walloomsac River, supplied the energy by which Sage's early mills were able to manufacture salable goods from raw materials. Around 1800, he turned his hand to other, more profitable materials and began producing iron. With his own son-in-law, Sage constructed new blast furnaces to the east of town in the section of Bennington still called Furnace Grove near the Woodford line. Sage continued in business until 1814, when he sold out and moved to New York State. He died in Pittsburgh two years later.

Through the marriages of his children, Sage and, therefore, Haviland are tied to several other prominent Bennington families. A daughter married into the town's populous Colvin family; a granddaughter became the wife of North Bennington's Martin Scott; and the successful local industrialist Olin Scott was their son.

North Bennington continued to ebb and flow as an industrial center throughout the nineteenth century. The stretch of Water Street now occupied by only a few functioning factories and a small number of homes once teemed with factory life and was filled with associated shops, taverns and other amusements. In time, North Bennington became the home of nationally known manufacturers of stereopticons; children's toys, such as the Kiddie Kar; and popular furniture. The Burden Iron Company, the H.C. White Company and the H.T. Cushman Furniture Company are only a few of the prominent company names that once called North Bennington home. One manufacturer of optical lenses and two other substantial mills were sited on the millpond that still lies near the center of town. Only one of those buildings now survives. A large shoe factory once stood in the center of town, where the small but elegant public library is today.

Economic trends, the transition to steam and then electric power and the concentration of labor and capital at the center of Bennington later attracted larger factories, but Bennington's North Village retains much of its independence and spirit from the days of Haviland and Sage.

ISAAC TICHENOR

1754–1838

Isaac Tichenor served as Vermont's governor twice in the early years of the state. He was elected the state's third and fifth governor, each term lasting one year. Tichenor, sometimes spelled "Tichnor," was born in Newark, New Jersey, on February 8, 1754. For that reason, as well as his good manners and dapper appearance, he was nicknamed locally "Jersey Slick." It has been suggested that he was also "slick" in terms of being sly and underhandedly clever. He was certainly intelligent, and when he graduated from Princeton University in 1775, he went to Schenectady to study law.

It was then that the Revolutionary War broke out, and Tichenor was appointed assistant commissary general for the Continental army. In that capacity, he came to Bennington to purchase supplies for the troops in the days leading up to the battle of August 16, 1777. In fact, he was the person responsible for filling the storehouses that General Burgoyne sent Colonel Baum to seize. A story handed down through the years is that Tichenor came to the Walloomsac Inn the day after the battle and was refused a meal by innkeeper Elijah Dewey's wife, Eunice, because she didn't know who he was and thought he should have been at the battlefield with the troops. Despite this harsh welcome to Bennington, Isaac decided to settle here and make it his home for the rest of his life. He became a captain in the local militia, served throughout the war and later became a major general.

Around 1790, Tichenor built the house that still stands behind the Walloomsac Inn on West Street. With its broad front lawn, it is one of the largest and most elegant houses in town, befitting a future governor. Inside the house, there is still a panel of the original wallpaper that was given to Tichenor after the death of Washington in 1799. It depicts a proposed memorial to the first president. Throughout his life in Bennington, Tichenor was involved in public projects. He was on the building committee formed to erect a new courthouse after the first one burned to the ground in 1809. Earlier, in 1804, he had also been on the committee charged with building the new church that is now called the Old First Church. Tichenor donated the bell for the church, but when it cracked, he made certain that a sturdy new one replaced it in 1823.

Tichenor was elected to the Vermont House of Representatives in 1781 and served as speaker two years later. During these years in the House, he also represented the independent Republic of Vermont in Washington and worked to have it admitted to the Union. In 1789, Isaac was active on the commission that settled the terms of an agreement with New York over the property disputes from two decades earlier. After Vermont's statehood was granted, Tichenor held a seat on the Vermont Supreme Court from 1791 to 1796. He left the bench in 1796 to become a member of the U.S. Senate but resigned that office in 1797 when he became the governor of Vermont. His party loyalty was with the Federalist Party and Alexander Hamilton, but he was left behind when Vermont slowly moved away from its support of a strong national government and became a Democratic-Republican state.

When he was once again elected to the United States Senate in 1815, Tichenor held his last public office. He served until 1821. He retired from political life but remained active in the community. He was a leader of the Temple Lodge of the Masons and was generally well liked by his neighbors. He was a man who loved hunting and fishing, and there are many stories about him that read like tall tales. One story recounts Tichenor shooting a deer through the window of his house while sitting inside in his easy chair. Another tale says that he and a friend bet on who could catch the most trout. When they weighed the fish, Tichenor had lost. Disappointed, he said to his friend that he didn't see how he could have won since Tichenor had filled his fish with gravel, to which his friend said, "I was too much for you this time—I stuffed mine with shot." The governor died in his Bennington home on December 11, 1838, at the age of eighty-four.

ANTHONY HASWELL

1756–1816

Bennington's Anthony Haswell was the first in a long and distinguished line of publishers, editors, journalists and writers to be associated with the area. He is also among its most celebrated figures.

Born in Portsmouth, England, on April 6, 1756, Anthony Haswell and his brother William were brought to this country by their father, a ship's carpenter, in 1770. His brother and father soon returned home, but Anthony stayed as an apprentice to a potter in Boston, where he had relatives. While his family's British ties later caused them difficulties, Anthony immediately began to show signs of the political and social temper that would forever mark his character. He witnessed the Boston Massacre and possibly Boston's famous Tea Party. His cousin Susanna Haswell, on the Loyalist side of his family, using the pen name "Mrs. Rowson," became the author of the novel *Charlotte Temple* and other popular books.

On July 23, 1771, in pursuit of employment that would allow him to express his strong views, Haswell apprenticed himself to the respected Boston printer Isaiah Thomas. In 1775, he moved to Worcester, and in 1776–77, he served in the army of the new nation. Between 1777 and 1782, he produced publications of his own, including *Haswell's Massachusetts Spy*, the newspaper he took over from Thomas in 1777, and the *New England Almanac*, published in Worcester in 1781 (though it was actually printed in Hartford). In 1781, he lived in Hartford and then moved to Springfield, Massachusetts, a year later.

The Vermont Gazette.

While DECENCY *and* CANDOR *guide the* PEN——*Our* PRESS *ſhall* SCORN *the* IMPERIOUS FROWN *of* MEN.

VOLUME VIII.] MONDAY, APRIL 18, 1791. [NUMBER 47.

Printed and publiſhed (every MONDAY) by ANTHONY HASWELL, at his office, a few rods ſouth of the courthouſe, BENNINGTON.

The beautiful and noted

HORSE,

WILDAIR,

WILL cover, the enſuing ſeaſon, at the ſtables of Simonds and Stewart, in Williamſtown. He is a bright bay coloured horſe, full blooded, about 15 hands high; is noted for a horſe of good carriage, and getting beautiful, active colts; he will perform his buſineſs at the moderate price of twelve ſhillings the ſingle leap, in caſh, or ready pay, or four dollars the ſeaſon; conſtant attendance will be given, and good paſturing for mares. It is expected that thoſe gentlemen who wiſh to have their mares go for the ſeaſon, will pay in grain, delivered to either of the ſubſcribers, by the firſt day of February next; otherwiſe in caſh.

☞ It is requeſted that thoſe gentlemen who improved the horſe laſt ſeaſon, would remit their ſeveral balances, as ſoon as may be, to oblige the public's humble ſervants,

SIMONDS and STEWART.

Williamſtown, March 30, 1791. 45

Miſcellany.

From the CONNECTICUT COURANT.

THE PROMPTER.

To the Prompter—*ſir,*
How ſhould I work it?

ARE you a parent? Then you have a hard taſk to be both the *friend* and the *maſter* of your children; and if you are not *both, you do not work it* [...]

[...] loſes the little authority that he had over the child—the order of things is changed—the child is the maſter, and when the child has been maſter a few months, you may as well break his *neck*, as his *will*. A thouſand laſhes, on a young *maſter's* back, will not do ſo much as one *deciſive command*, before he becomes *maſter* of his parent.

Now liſten to my advice—the idea is *new*. A child does not regard ſo much what a parent ſays, as how he ſays it. A child looks at his parent's eye when he ſpeaks—and then he reads intuitively what his parent means, and how much he means. If a parent ſpeaks with an *air of indifference, without emphaſis*, or looks another way when he ſpeaks, the child pays little or no regard to what he ſays. (I ſpeak of a young child over whom a parent has not yet eſtabliſhed an authority.) But if a parent, when he commands a child to do or not to do, looks at him with the *eye of command*, and ſpeaks with a tone and air of deciſion and authority, the child is impreſſed with this manner of commanding, and will ſeldom venture to diſobey. A ſteady uniform authority of this kind, which never varies from its purpoſe, which never gives way to the caprices or appetites of children, which carries every command into effect, will prevent the neceſſity of a rod. I am bold to ſay, that a parent who has this ſteady authority, will never have occaſion to correct a child of common ſenſibility—*and never but once*, a child of uncommon obſtinacy. This is the way every parent and maſter ſhould work it.

But the common practice is, for a parent to throw away his own authority, and become the ſlave of his children; and when the young maſters grow headſtrong, and commit all manner of miſchief, then the parent complains of old Adam, original ſin, and the devil—and ſwears he'll drive the devil out, or he'll *know the reaſon why*. Then for the *fiſt* and the *rod*.

[...] line in his face writes abſtinence;—every ſtride looks like a check upon his deſires: ſee, I beſeech you, how he is cloak'd up with ſermons, prayers, & ſacraments; and ſo bemuffled with the externals of religion, that he has not a hand to ſpare for a worldly purpoſe;—he has armour at leaſt—Why does he put it on? Is there no ſerving God without all this? Muſt the garb of religion be extended ſo wide to the danger of its rending?—Yes, truly, or it will not hide the ſecret—and, what is that?—That the ſaint has no religion at all.

OSTENTATIOUS GENEROSITY.

———BUT here comes generoſity; giving—not to a decayed artiſt—but to the arts and ſciences themſelves.——See—he *builds not a chamber in the wall apart for the prophet*; but whole ſchools and colleges for thoſe who come after. Lord! how they will magnify his name! 'tis in capitals already; the firſt—the higheſt, in the gilded rentroll of every hoſpital and aſylum.——

——One honeſt tear ſhed in private over the unfortunate, is worth it all.

For the GAZETTE.

Mr. HASWELL,

Pleaſe to inſert the following APHORISMS *in your gazette.*

AS deliberate counſel is to mobs: ſo is honeſty to electioneering.

The former brings the mob back to government.

The latter brings the electioneerer back to his oath.

Amongſt republican legiſlators a certain degree of jealouſy and reſerve is ſalutary: whilſt intimacy and combination are deſtructive.

Wicked men, and even devils, would make good legiſlators, were jealouſy to take her ſeat amongſt them.

The *Vermont Gazette*, published by Anthony Haswell. *Bennington Museum, Bennington, VT.*

In the spring of 1783, Haswell was invited to Bennington, then the political and social center of Vermont, to start a newspaper. As a further inducement to stay, he was made postmaster general of the independent Republic of Vermont in 1784 and was offered a large share of the republic's official printing. He accepted, and these appointments made his life here more financially feasible. His *Vermont Gazette* became Vermont's first successful newspaper after a smaller publication, also called *The Gazette*, failed. The *Vermont Gazette* began its publication in June 1783 and continued in various forms over the succeeding years.

During his thirty-year residence in Bennington, Haswell became well known and influential due to his strong commitments to the political and social issues of the day. He had a decisive effect on the cultural development of the town through his newspaper. Within the growing Haswell family, he had seventeen children with two different wives; daily family gatherings were directed toward "mental and moral improvement." Emphasizing Haswell's dominant local role as a publisher, one historian points out that many area libraries were made up largely of works Haswell himself printed. Because of his work, many visitors to the region, such as the well-known clergyman Reverend Nathan Perkins, who toured Vermont in 1789, found the literary and cultural life of the state to be strongest in Bennington.

Haswell enjoyed a long and productive career. In 1792, he founded the first newspaper in Rutland called the *Herald of Rutland.* Unfortunately, the printing office burned to the ground after only a few issues had been published. He also published Ethan Allen's querulous tract on belief, *Reason: The Only Oracle of Man*, and reprinted Tom Paine's *The Rights of Man*. His full bibliography runs some fifty pages of books, pamphlets, periodicals and broadsides. Haswell died in Bennington on May 26, 1816, and was buried in the Old Bennington Cemetery.

He is best known for his challenge to the Alien and Sedition Acts, passed by Congress in July 1798, first in defense of representative Matthew Lyon of Arlington, who was the earliest victim of the acts, and later himself, when he was imprisoned. He forcefully defended free speech and the freedom of the press. He published the details of Lyon's imprisonment and assisted in raising funds for his release. Lyon became the only member of Congress to be elected to office while serving time in prison. When Haswell himself was arrested two years later on similar charges, he wrote:

And if truth is a libel—Alas! and alas!
May the spirit of seventy-five
Again be enkindled—A toast—let it pass!
For who would his freedom survive.

JOHN NORTON

1758–1828

Bennington has long been associated with the production of pottery. John Norton was the first in a long line of potters, which continues up to the present day. Norton, a native of Goshen, Connecticut, arrived in Bennington about 1785 after a short stay in nearby Williamstown, Massachusetts. A farmer and a veteran of the Revolutionary War, Norton bought a large farm south of Bennington Center on what is now called Monument Avenue Extension. In 1793, after working eight years as a farmer, he set up his first kiln for the manufacture of stoneware as a small cottage industry.

For many years, the Norton pottery was a modest family business that operated out of their family farm. Norton was aided in the business by his son Luman Norton (1785–1858) and a nephew, Norman Judd. They produced the practical and durable redware that was commonly made by smaller New England potteries of the time.

In 1823, Luman and his brother John Jr. took over the pottery. Eventually, Luman came to oversee the entire enterprise, increasing production, especially of the salt-glazed stoneware and Rockingham ware for which the business became particularly well known. Today, the large crocks and jugs manufactured during this era, often with boldly painted decorations, are widely collected.

In 1828, the year Captain John Norton died, the Norton operation partnered with the Fenton brothers, successful potters from Dorset, who brought new talents and expertise into the business's production and designs.

The earliest piece of Norton pottery known to exist was made for Omindia Armstrong. *Bennington Museum, Bennington, VT.*

The partnership was sealed by the marriage of one of the Fenton brothers, Christopher, to the daughter of Luman Norton.

By the early 1830s, the Norton and Fenton pottery kilns had been relocated to larger quarters on what is now Park Street in downtown Bennington, then aptly called Pottery Street. In the years after 1847, with the help of a British designer, Daniel Greatbach, Fenton expanded his line of products to include Parian ware and other more refined, decorative products. These more ornate, highly colored, delicately crafted works included pieces with animal themes and fancy pitchers. A selection of this type of work, exhibited under the name of the United States Pottery Company, was shown to great acclaim at the New York Crystal Palace exhibition in 1853.

Fenton's ambitious United States Pottery Company remained in business only until 1858, but the Norton pottery, with its more utilitarian ware, continued in production until the 1890s. Thus, the craftsmanship of John Norton left Bennington with a legacy of ceramic products that played a strong role in the town's economy and its eventual recognition as a center of industry and design. Although not directly related to the Norton and Fenton industries, today's Bennington Pottery on County Street has carried on the tradition of ceramics for over seventy-five years.

SIPP IVES

UNKNOWN–1777

It will probably surprise many readers that one of the members of the Green Mountain Boys who fought and died at the Battle of Bennington was Black. In fact, recent research has shown that there were at least six Black men who took part in the battle, and one of those men was killed that day. His name was Scipio "Sipp" Ives. A historian from Stockbridge, Massachusetts, Lion G. Miles, spent many years trying to identify the names of the soldiers and militia members on both sides of the battle, and his discoveries brought to light some previously unknown names, including Ives's. Very little is known about Sipp beyond his military service history. We don't even know where or when he was born.

Sipp Ives appears to have been living in or around Cheshire, Massachusetts, a village that, at the time, was called New Providence, on February 14, 1777, when he volunteered for three years of active duty with Seth Warner's Continental regiment of Green Mountain Boys. No records indicate whether he was enslaved or free at the time of his enlistment. It was common for enslavers to send one of their enslaved men into the military in their place. We do know that Captain Abiathar Angel recruited Ives, along with a few other men, as a private that day. Two of those other recruits were also Black, the brothers Simeon and Charles Grandison.

Ives was part of a contingent of men under Colonel Seth Warner's command who were sent to replace the men stationed at Fort Ticonderoga, as their terms of enlistment were expiring. Ives's militia patrolled the area below Otter Creek until they were forced to retreat, outnumbered by the superior British forces advancing from Canada to retake Ticonderoga on July 5, 1777. The bulk of the Patriots fell back, with Warner's men acting as a rear guard, fighting the Battle of Hubbardton to delay the British during the Americans' strategic retreat. During this action, Warner's regiment suffered heavy casualties, and hundreds were captured. They fell back as far as Manchester, where they awaited further orders. On August 14, General Stark instructed the men to quickly march to Bennington, where they arrived just in the nick of time. They routed the reinforcements sent by General Burgoyne, who were commanded by Colonel Breymann, and ensured the Patriot victory in the Battle of Bennington. During the battle, Sipp Ives was mortally wounded and died the following day, August 17, 1777. Sipp's body was identified on the battlefield by Captain Daniel Brown of Lanesborough. It is not known for certain, but Ives was probably buried with other soldiers on the battlefield in an unmarked grave.

BENJAMIN HARWOOD AND HIRAM HARWOOD

1762–1851 AND 1788–1839

One of the historical treasures of the Bennington Museum is an extensive set of diaries kept by two of the town's early residents. Their views of local and sometimes broader events provide us with a direct window into an earlier time.

Benjamin and Hiram Harwood, father and son, were farmers on the south end of Bennington at a time when the town was largely rural and community ties were close. Benjamin Harwood, born on January 12, 1762, is believed to have been the first non-Native child born in Bennington. Benjamin's parents, Peter and Margaret Harwood, arrived with Benjamin's grandmother Bridget Harwood with the first settlers in 1761. Bridget was reputed to have spurred her horse to a gallop in order to be the first to arrive. On November 8, 1762, she was also destined to be the first adult to die in the new settlement.

The family immediately went to work to establish a farm, and once Hiram was born, he continued his father's work on the farm. Hiram did not succeed Benjamin, as the son predeceased the father by more than a decade. The elder Harwood began keeping a diary in 1805, and his son continued making daily entries until 1837. Thus, these diaries are viewed as a joint endeavor. Through the thirty-year lens of the diaries, life in Bennington during the early decades of the nineteenth century comes alive. They faithfully recorded the cycle of farming, the pattern of regular community events, outstanding news and the occasional unusual occurrence. The personal tone of the diaries lends immediacy to these experiences. Perusing these volumes through the

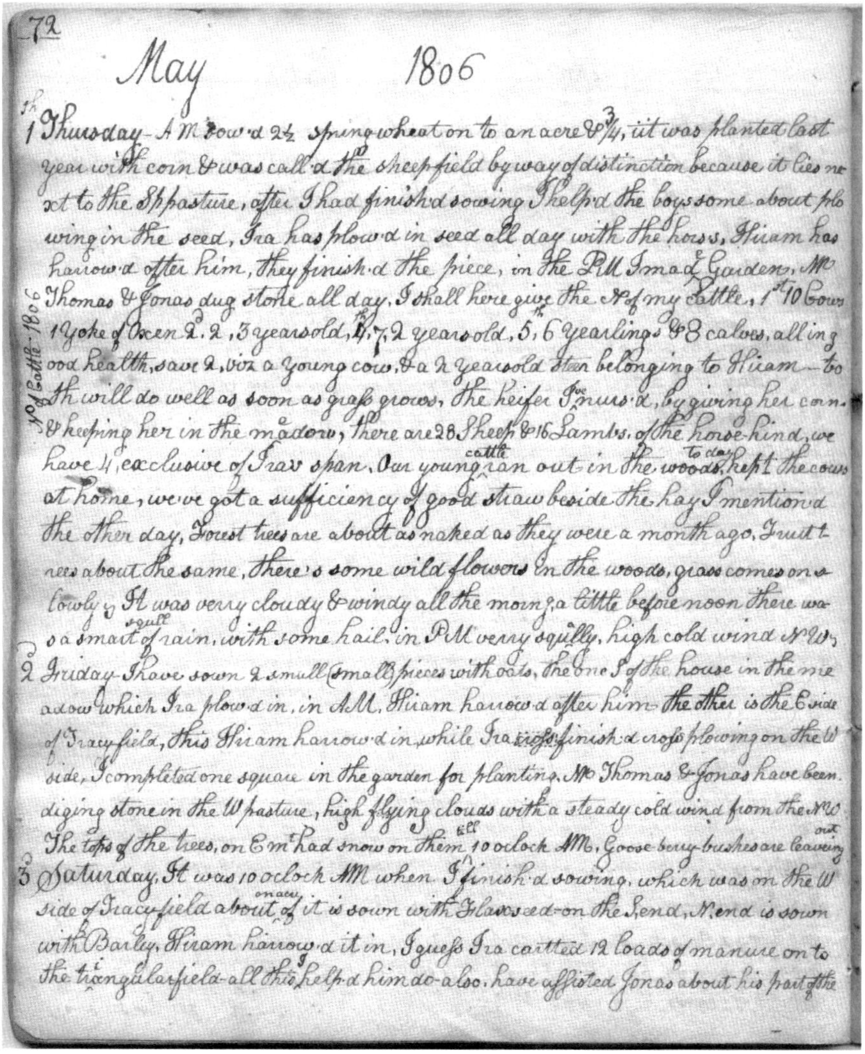
72

May 1806

1st Thursday—A M sow'd 2½ spring wheat on to an acre & 3/4, it was planted last
year with corn & was call'd the sheep field by way of distinction because it lies ne
xt to the Sp pasture, after I had finish'd sowing I help'd the boys some about plo
wing in the seed, Ira has plow'd in seed all day with the horss, Hiram has
harrow'd after him, they finish'd the piece, in the P.M. I made Garden, Mr
Thomas & Jonas dug stone all day. I shall here give the No of my Cattle, 1st 10 Cows
1 Yoke of Oxen 2d. 2, 3 years old, 4th. 7, 2 years old, 5th. 6 Yearlings & 8 calves, all in g
ood health, save 2, viz a young cow, & a 2 year old steer belonging to Hiram—bo
th will do well as soon as grass grows, the heifer I've nurs'd, by giving her corn
& keeping her in the meadow, there are 28 Sheep & 16 Lambs, of the horse kind, we
have 4, exclusive of Ira's span. Our young cattle ran out in the woods to day, kept the cows
at home, we've got a sufficiency of good straw beside the hay I mention'd
the other day, Forest trees are about as naked as they were a month ago, Fruit t-
rees about the same, there's some wild flowers in the woods, grass comes on s
lowly. It was verry cloudy & windy all the morn, a little before noon there wa
s a smart squall of rain, with some hail, in P.M. verry squally, high cold wind N.W.
2d Friday—I have sown 2 small (small) pieces with oats, the one S of the house in the me
adow which Ira plow'd in, in A.M. Hiram harrow'd after him—the other is the E side
of Tracy field, this Hiram harrow'd in, while Ira finish'd cross plowing on the W
side, I completed one square in the garden for planting. Mr Thomas & Jonas have been
diging stone in the W pasture, high flying clouds with a steady cold wind from the N.W.
The tops of the trees, on E mt had snow on them till 10 oclock AM, Goose berry bushes are leaving out
3 Saturday, It was 10 oclock AM when I finish'd sowing, which was on the W
side of Tracy field about an acre of it is sown with Flax seed—on the S end, N end is sown
with Barley, Hiram harrow'd it in, I guess Ira carted 12 loads of manure on to
the triangular field—all this I help'd him do—also, have afsisted Jonas about his part of the

[margin: No of Cattle 1806]

A page from the Harwood Diaries, May 1806. *Bennington Museum, Bennington, VT.*

various years, we can trace the routines of plowing, planting, cultivation and harvest. We learn of illnesses and deaths, engagements, births, parties and other celebrations. Visitors to town are noted, and current events are either endorsed or disapproved of.

Early in 1806, the dedication of the new meetinghouse, Bennington's famous Old First Church, is recorded. Its builders are listed along with its cost and the length of time it took to complete it—June 25, 1804, to December

31, 1805. The subject of the first sermon is identified: 2 Samuel, chapter 24, and 2 Chronicles, chapter 5. Personal items are noted. For instance, on New Year's Day 1811, we are told that Hiram played the flute at a party at the house of his neighbor Captain John Norton. Hiram even confesses that he was not entirely pleased with his performance that day.

In 1812, there is considerable discussion of the war with England and Hiram's somewhat unwilling service in the militia. It seems to have been a war that was less than popular among the residents of Bennington. The opinions Hiram read about in the few available periodicals are recorded. The diaries note local concerns in February that year. In particular, he mentions the melt-off from a winter thaw that carried away all the bridges on a long stretch of the Hoosic River. Entries for much of 1816 speak to New England's "year without a summer." It was in the spring of that year that the weather turned sour. There was snow through May and June and frost in July and August. With few successful crops, seed was expensive, and food supplies ran low. In a dramatic turn, the next winter proved to be remarkably mild.

Planting, cultivating, threshing, visits to the mill, replenishing the ever-present woodpile, the surprise arrival of a visiting carriage—all of this is life in a different era. The Harwood diaries even reveal the first attempts by Hiram's neighbor John Norton to set up a pottery. Bennington is extremely fortunate that the writings of such devoted chroniclers have been preserved. The Harwoods' penchant for noting the events and feelings of their day translates into a direct and vibrant message to readers today. Excerpts from the complete diary have been edited by Robert E. Shalhope and published in book form as *A Tale of New England.*

LAVIUS FILLMORE

1767–1850

In our time of multiculturalism and a diversity of beliefs, it may be difficult to conceive of the strife rampant among the various Protestant sects in early New England. Disputes over what might seem like small differences of interpretation of certain Bible passages could drive groups of worshipers to establish their own churches. Bennington, in fact, was founded by a separatist group of Congregationalists known as the New Lights. At the turn of the nineteenth century, friction among citizens who did or did not believe in a strict division between church and state led to disputes about whether or not taxpayers should pay for repairs to Bennington's decaying meetinghouse. Interestingly, Bennington's citizens were divided over the issue of the alleged religious infidelity of Thomas Jefferson. While Jefferson is today an icon of freedom, at that time, he was far too free a thinker for some in the Bennington community.

On January 30, 1804, two and a half years after the departure of Reverend Job Swift and before a new minister was selected, a building committee was appointed to plan a new meetinghouse for Bennington. The committee was composed of Isaac Tichenor, Jesse Field, Moses Robinson Jr. and Thomas Abel. A notice for building proposals was posted in the *Vermont Gazette*, and Oliver Abel Jr. and Lavius Fillmore, a team from Norwich, Connecticut, were chosen to design and build the new structure. Oliver was the brother of the building committee's Thomas Abel. Lavius was the nephew of Nathaniel Fillmore, a Bennington Patriot, farmer and grandfather of the future president Millard Fillmore. Lavius, a joiner, and Abel, a carpenter,

Old First Church, designed by Lavius Fillmore in 1804. *Photograph by Bill Morgan.*

were accompanied by Asa Hyde, also from Norwich, the carver responsible for the church's fine capitals and other graceful details.

Lavius Fillmore was born in Norwich in 1767 and was drawn to a career as a joiner, or finish carpenter. He soon became a designer of churches as well. Through the example of the Bennington meetinghouse and other later works, it is obvious that Fillmore had studied the details of buildings in Boston, Providence and other New England locations. He absorbed the style that Charles Bulfinch and Joseph Brown had adapted to New England. It came from the Palladian and Classical designs popularized by Christopher Wren and Robert Adam in Great Britain. Architects now believe that Fillmore was influenced by the American pattern book maker Asher Benjamin, whose book *The Country Builder's Assistant* he must have known.

Before coming to Bennington at the behest of the committee in 1804, Fillmore had completed Connecticut churches in East Haddam, Middletown and Norwich. Although he had worked for little more than a decade, he was already an acknowledged master of building and design in a sophisticated style that was not only outstanding in its own right but would also influence generations of architects in the future. Bennington's Old First Church, designed and built by Fillmore between 1804 and 1806, is still one of the town's principal attractions. It is one of the most beautiful examples of a Federal-style meetinghouse in New England, with an unusually elegant and harmonious combination of the American, British and Palladian elements for which these buildings are known. Although it was substantially altered to become a Victorian church over the course of the nineteenth century, the Old First Church was carefully restored in 1937 by Bennington's indefatigable Reverend Vincent Ravi-Booth. Today, thanks to Booth, the boxed seats, whose sale financed the building of the church; the original vaulted ceiling; the large clear windows; and the dramatic raised pulpit can again be seen as they were originally designed by Fillmore.

After 1806, Fillmore and his family moved on to Middlebury, where other examples of his work still stand. Other examples of Fillmore's influence can still be found in Bennington homes that were built or modified at that time. These are recognizable by their Palladian windows and other features reminiscent of the Old First Church. For the rest of his life, Fillmore remained in Middlebury, where he continued his active life in carpentry, milling and design. He died there in 1850.

DANIEL HARMON AND ELIZABETH HARMON

1778–1843 AND CIRCA 1790–1862

The stories of Daniel and Elizabeth "Lizette" Duval Harmon and Simon Fraser are among the most extraordinary and romantic in the history of Bennington. They reveal how the town was tied through family and destiny to the larger currents of the continent and the era.

Born in Bennington, Daniel Williams Harmon was the son of Captain Daniel Harmon and his wife, Lucretia. The elder Harmon had fought with the Bennington militia under Captain Elijah Dewey, who was both Lucretia's cousin and the son of Bennington's minister Jedediah Dewey. Like many early Bennington settlers, the Harmons were Separatists, austere Calvinists of Puritanical faith and strict views. They were the proprietors of Harmons' Tavern, which once stood near today's intersection of Vail and Airport Roads. It was a well-known hostelry in the early days and was reportedly where General Stark had his breakfast en route to the Battle of Bennington. The tavern is long gone and remembered by only a small plaque today.

Shortly before 1800, the younger Daniel left Bennington and went to work in Montreal as a clerk in the fur trade for McTavish, Frobisher and Company. Before long, he found himself in the employ of the North West Company, a new and growing competitor to the older and more established Hudson's Bay Company. In 1800, he signed a seven-year contract as a field agent for the company. It was his job to oversee trade with Native and French Canadian trappers and supply the company's trading posts in the West.

In this capacity, Harmon spent most of the next twenty years in the far reaches of western Canada, penetrating deep into unknown territory and

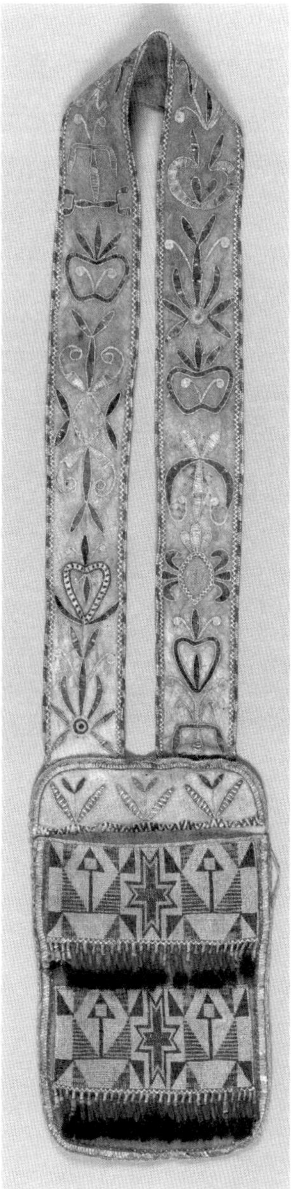

Shot bag made by Elizabeth Harmon. *Bennington Museum, Bennington, VT.*

often remaining there for long periods. His principal informants and companions were Native peoples. Some eight and a half years of this time he spent in the virtually unknown territory west of the Rocky Mountains.

Through his perseverance and ability, Harmon became one of the most successful of the North West Company's traders and was eventually made a partner. His observations, gleaned from travel, exploration and communication with the region's Native population became important sources for the mapmakers of the day. On his return to the East, he published a memoir of his travels titled *A Journal of Voyages and Travels in the Interior of North America*, along with other works on the wildlife and Native peoples of northwestern Canada. Though he became known as an explorer, Harmon's business and religious concerns seem to have taken precedence over any interest in personal recognition. He is believed to have come within one hundred miles of the Pacific Ocean without, apparently, having felt the need to see it for himself.

In 1805, after considerable soul searching dictated by his Bennington Christian upbringing, Harmon formed an alliance with a woman from the Cree tribe whose father had been a French Canadian trader. Such relationships were far from uncommon in Harmon's time. Unlike many of his peers, however, Harmon remained allied to Lizette throughout his life, taught her his strict brand of Christianity and formally married her upon their return to Vermont. In 1820, they settled with other members of the Harmon family in Coventry, Vermont.

Despite earlier success and substantial wealth, Daniel, Lizette and their ten children led a life of increasing difficulty and financial peril.

Daniel, virtually unknown despite his accomplishments, along with three of his children, died of smallpox in 1843. Lizette lived on, though in difficult financial circumstances, until 1862. Their youngest daughter, the proprietor for many years of a successful school for girls in Ottawa, died by suicide at the age of sixty-six. Her rather unusual request was to be buried in the same grave as her mother in Montreal's Mount Royal Cemetery.

MARTIN SCOTT

1788–1847

The general renown for Colonel Martin Scott of Bennington is centered on his skill as a marksman and military hero. Born in Bennington on January 17, 1788, Scott was raised on a farm west of town. Though he spent his youth doing farm labor, he was noted for his abilities as a hunter and for the accuracy with which he could handle a rifle. Like Davy Crockett, he is said to have shot his first bear when he was a young boy—in Scott's case, he was just thirteen. In the tradition of the American tall tale, Benningtonians of his day claimed that Scott had no need to hunt; the animals, when apprised of his approach, simply turned themselves over to him, knowing that flight was useless.

Such myths were based on a certain amount of truth. After accepting a commission in the U.S. Army, Scott was, according to local lore, soon acknowledged as one of the best shots in the entire army. Having enlisted during the War of 1812, by 1814, he had been commissioned a second lieutenant, then promoted to first lieutenant in 1819 and to captain in 1828. In 1846, he was made a major and, finally, a lieutenant colonel.

His military career, spent mostly in remote and romantic-sounding locations on the western frontier, Florida and, later, Mexico, lent luster to his image back home. According to several accounts, Scott was disliked by his fellow officers, but he cut a dashing figure on his visits to relatives in Bennington. He arrived home after his posting in the West with two fine horses, a fancy carriage, a pack of dogs and a young serving boy in livery. At a time in which neither wealth nor luxuries were commonplace in town, Scott's visit created an unforgettable impression.

Martin Scott. *Bennington Museum, Bennington, VT.*

A career like Scott's also exposed him to danger on a regular basis. His comrades in combat must have noted his enthusiasm for his work with mixed emotion. "Martin Scott never stoops in battle," is said to have been his oft-used motto. But a man's prominence in battle creates a target for the enemy as well as loyalty from one's own brigade. After showing heroism in the Battles of Palo Alto, Resaca de la Palma and Monterey, Scott took a blow to the chest on September 8, 1847, at the Battle of Molino del Rey and died within an hour.

His body was returned from Mexico and arrived in Bennington in February 1848. On March 2, 1848, a lavish military funeral was held in town with more than five thousand people in attendance. The procession included many organizations, both local and regional. A notable feature was a riderless horse, the same one on which Scott had arrived in Bennington on an earlier visit. Mourning flags bearing the legend "Molino del Rey" were draped over his hearse.

Colonel Scott was buried in Old Bennington Cemetery in the company of his many family members who had been early settlers of the area. His monument speaks of his bravery and long service; he was nearly sixty when he died in battle. In marksmanship, Colonel Scott had certainly found the career that suited him best and proved to be useful to his country, for which his fellow townsmen took pleasure in honoring him. Fort Martin Scott in Texas was named in his honor.

JOEL VALENTINE AND ALONZO BUCKINGHAM VALENTINE

1791–1866 AND 1830–1904

The Valentine family first settled in Bennington in 1822, and within two years, Joel Valentine had purchased a fulling mill on the banks of the Walloomsac River and went into the woolen cloth business for himself. Valentine was born on January 22, 1791, in a town in nearby Washington County, New York, where he grew up on a farm. As frequently happened in nineteenth-century Bennington, a fire struck his first mill, and it was destroyed in 1836. He resumed his business in temporary quarters until he was able to build a new brick factory on Pleasant Street. Originally, the mill produced woolen goods, but in the 1860s, after Valentine's son Alonzo Valentine took over the business, it was converted into a cotton mill. For a while, it was the largest mill in the state and employed more than 150 workers. It produced ladies' vests and drawers made of white-, scarlet- and natural-colored cotton and wool. Kerosene lamps were used for lighting the mill so they could work at night, but just as the building was being fitted for a more modern gasoline lighting system, the Bradford mill gas lighting system blew up. That put a quick end to Valentine's idea.

Boys and girls worked in the mill for $0.75 to $1.25 per day, while the managers might have made as much as $4 per day. Most of the labor was provided by young girls and women whose fingers were nimble enough to tie and maintain the threads that fed into the machinery. To make the plant more cheerful and pleasant, paintings and engravings were hung on the factory walls. Once again, in the early 1880s, the Valentine mills were destroyed by fire, and once again, they were rebuilt, this time with even

Major Alonzo B. Valentine.
Bennington Museum, Bennington, VT.

newer firefighting equipment and a tall clock tower and bell that struck the hours and sounded alarms.

Joel's son Alonzo Valentine, born in Bennington on April 1, 1830, was adventurous as a young man. After attending school at the Union Academy a few blocks away on Union Street, Alonzo headed west in 1852, hoping to strike it rich in the gold fields. He made some money there, but by no means did he find the fortune he was searching for. Then he spent two years in Wisconsin, where he purchased a lumber camp. On July 31, 1862, he enlisted in the Tenth Regiment of the Vermont Volunteers, and he remained in the army until the end of the Civil War. He saw action in the Battles of the Wilderness, Spotsylvania, Cold Harbor, Fishers Hill and, finally, Petersburg. It was only then that Alonzo gave up his wanderlust and returned to Bennington. He went back into the knitting business following his father's 1866 death.

As a mill owner, Alonzo Valentine became one of the town's major philanthropists. He lived in his family's house on Pleasant Street, just in front of his mill, and married Alma Park, a sister of Trenor Park, with whom he had four children. He was especially interested in providing a good education for the children of the community. Alonzo was quite active in the establishment of a graded school system, serving for ten years as a trustee, and he and his wife made generous donations toward the school's buildings and grounds. He was elected to the state senate in 1886 and held many posts within veteran organizations statewide, where he was known as Major Valentine. In later years, his business interests expanded to include the Bennington County Savings Bank, of which he became president. He even had time to act as vice president of the Bennington Battle Monument and Historical Society.

Of lasting importance was Alonzo's role in the establishment of the Vermont Veterans' Home in 1886. Alma was also active in town projects and did a lot to beautify the area. She helped enhance the park that once graced East Main Street near the entrance to the Village Cemetery. It was the only public park in town at the time and included a fine cast-iron fountain that everyone enjoyed on hot summer days. Now, that plot of land is unused, and the unattractive entrance to the cemetery is hidden around the corner on Morgan Street.

One interesting project that Valentine adopted was the idea to lure farmers from Sweden to Vermont. To implement the program, he was made commissioner of agriculture and manufacturing for the state. At the time, farms were being abandoned one by one, and the population of rural Vermont was dwindling. Valentine hoped that the trend would be reversed by the immigration of Swedes. They were "Protestants and thrifty and peaceable," he wrote. He felt that Swedes would assimilate faster than any other immigrants, and by this, he was probably voicing a popular opinion that Vermont had enough Roman Catholics in the state already and didn't need more. In 1890, about fifty-five Swedes landed in Philadelphia and made their way to agricultural areas near Wilmington, Weston and Vershire. The program was discontinued shortly thereafter, but some of the descendants of those families are still in the area today.

Sadly, Alonzo's life was filled with tragedies. On January 13, 1882, his twenty-two-year-old son, Park Valentine, died along with his young bride the day after their wedding in a terrible accident during their honeymoon. The train crash became known as the Spuyten Duyvil Railroad Disaster. Another son, Wells Valentine, also died at a young age. In 1902, the Valentine Mills ceased production and went out of business. At least Alonzo lived to see Willow Street (directly across from the mill) be renamed Valentine Street in honor of his father. Major Valentine died the following year, on July 9, 1904, at the age of seventy-four in his home at 304 Pleasant Street, where he had spent most of his life.

SILAS HAWES AND THE EAGLE SQUARE COMPANY

ACTIVE CIRCA 1812–1827

Shortly after the War of 1812, Shaftsbury blacksmith Silas Hawes conceived of the idea of welding two pieces of steel together at a ninety-degree angle to create the modern carpenter's square. His first attempt utilized two old sawblades that he had taken from a customer in trade. Although he began making the squares as early as 1814, it wasn't until December 15, 1819, that Hawes received his patent for the invention. Silas's background is a bit of a mystery, as no records seem to exist for either his birth or his death. He went into the business of manufacturing his carpenter's squares with Stephen Whipple, a fellow Shaftsbury blacksmith. New building and expansion in the early 1800s created such a strong market for the squares that in 1823, Whipple built the stone mill that is still visible at the junction of Routes 7A and 67A, just north of the center of South Shaftsbury, to meet the demand. There, the partners set up trip hammers powered by a waterwheel to make the squares. In 1825, Whipple and another partner bought some nearby land, which they leased to Hawes for a little over $100 a year. This was the beginning of the Eagle Square site, where carpenter's squares and other tools were manufactured for nearly two centuries.

Little else is known about Hawes, who retired from the business in 1827, but the manufacture of squares in Shaftsbury continued, as did his company but under other ownership. The business and plant were first sold to John Hastings of Hardwick, Massachusetts. When Hawes's patent expired in 1833, several new square shops opened in the area. Among them were those

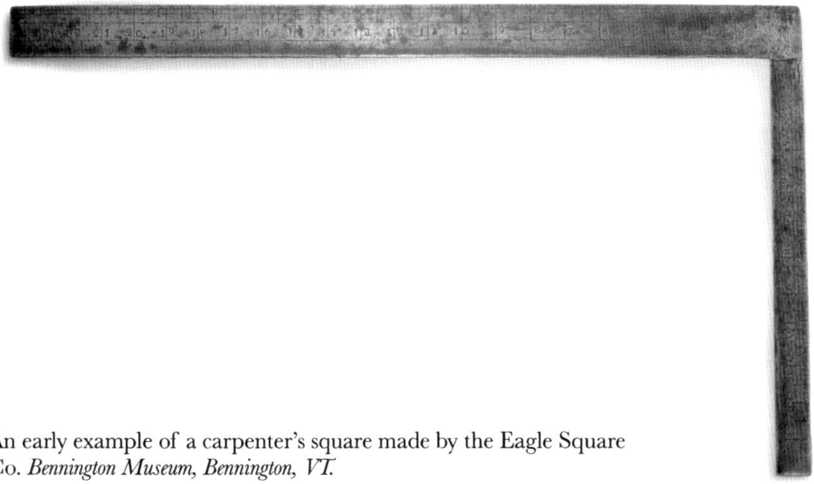

An early example of a carpenter's square made by the Eagle Square Co. *Bennington Museum, Bennington, VT.*

of Jeremiah Essex and Rufus Bangs in North Bennington and Norman Douglas and Stephen and Heman Whipple in Shaftsbury. Stephen Whipple was the son of Hawes's original partner.

In 1845, John Hastings was bought out by Dennis George. The improvements he brought to the making of squares created a need for more capital, a challenge met in 1859 by the formation of the Eagle Square Company, which brought George together with Essex, Bangs, Heman Whipple and some other local entrepreneurs. Under a variety of owners and managers, the company continued using the Eagle Square name well into the twentieth century. After 1860, the firm expanded its line of products; production lines were set up for wooden furniture, building supplies and parts for tools. To provide the wood for these items, the company acquired a large tract of forest land northeast of Bennington and operated two sawmills. By the 1880s, according to Ruth Levin, who has researched the history of Eagle Square, the company was producing thirty-five thousand wooden bedsteads a year in addition to its other products.

High production levels, innovative products and improved mechanization brought considerable success to Eagle Square. Over the years, it remained an important local employer, and through its high-quality products, it spread the names of Shaftsbury and Bennington far beyond the state's borders. It was in 1915 that the company was acquired by the Stanley Tool Company. By 1937, the Eagle Square plant employed about one hundred workers and produced some 190,000 carpenter's squares per year. In 1971, the plant was rebuilt and replaced with a new two-hundred-thousand-square-foot workspace. During the renovation, Hawes's original shop was restored, and by 1976, the total number of employees had peaked at nearly four hundred. Sadly, the plant closed in 2001.

Eagle Square is one of Bennington's great success stories. Through hard work, planning and the exigencies of many business cycles, it turned the legacy of an inventive Vermonter into a dynamic industrial base for the community. Though Silas Hawes himself was in business for only a brief period, his contributions to the economy of the area have been substantial and long-lasting.

HILAND HALL

1795–1885

In addition to being Vermont's governor from 1858 to 1860, Hiland Hall had a long and distinguished career in law and government and was the leading figure in many aspects of Bennington's civic and community affairs. In the years leading up to the Civil War, he was also a political player in both the Whig and Republican Parties on the larger national stage. In addition, he was widely known as one of Bennington's greatest historians.

Hall was born in Bennington on July 20, 1795, into a family with deep roots in New England. He was educated in local schools in North Bennington, at the time known as Sage's City, and spent two terms at an academy in Granville, New York. As a youth, Hall was known to be an avid reader. Following his basic education, he taught in district schools for several terms. Then he undertook the study of law with Bennington attorney Marshall Carter before he was admitted to the bar in June 1819.

Hall's accomplishments in the political sphere are legion, and there is almost no position he didn't fill at one time or another. Before he was twenty years old, he had become active in a patriotic organization known as the Sons of Liberty. By the early 1820s, he was the registrar for the Bennington Probate Court. He was next elected as a Vermont state representative in 1827 for one term and then appointed clerk of Bennington County from 1828 to 1829, while at the same time he served as state's attorney from 1828 to 1831. For another decade, from 1833 to 1843, he represented southern Vermont in Washington, D.C., at the U.S. House of Representatives. Returning to Vermont from 1843 to 1846, he became the state's bank commissioner and

Hiland Hall. *Bennington Museum, Bennington, VT.*

then a judge on its supreme court from 1846 to 1850. From 1850 to 1851, he returned to Washington to work as the second comptroller of the United States Treasury. Between 1851 and 1854, he served in the newly formed state of California as chairman of the state land commission, a position to which he had been appointed by President Fillmore. To do this, he had to sell his farm animals and equipment in Bennington and move west. Once in California, he busied himself trying to settle the thousands of land claims and border disputes that resulted from the acquisition of the territory from Mexico. After the death of his son Hiland H. Hall, who had made the trip to California with him, he asked his son-in-law, Trenor Park, in Bennington to join him on the West Coast. Park jumped at the opportunity and used his law background to build a quick fortune through the management of the Mariposa gold mines among other lucrative endeavors. In the meantime, Hall lost his position in California with the land commission when Franklin Pierce was elected president, so he returned to Bennington in 1854.

On his arrival back east, Hall once again settled into the practice of law and participation in politics. In 1856, he was a representative to the first presidential convention of the Republican Party held in Philadelphia, where John C. Fremont of California was nominated, only to lose to the Democratic Party nominee, James Buchanan. Two years later, in 1858 and 1859, Hall was elected to two successive one-year terms as governor of Vermont, the high point of his political career.

In his civic life, as witnessed by the positions he held, Hall was widely respected for his probity and thoroughness. His tenure in Congress was reported to be more focused on problem-solving than on the declamatory speeches favored by his colleagues. He took a strong position against slavery and played an important role in reorganizing the Department of the Post Office. Through his own initiative, he investigated an extensive set of fraudulent Revolutionary War claims against the government, which would have cost the taxpayers a substantial amount. Following his two terms as governor, Hall was sent to Washington as the chairman of the delegation to the Peace Conference of 1861, aimed at preventing the Civil War.

In 1863, Hiland Hall's son-in-law, Trenor Park, returned from California, where he had amassed a fortune. Trenor bought Hall's farm in North Bennington for $20,000, and before long, Hiland and Dolly moved into an apartment in the new mansion Park built for himself on the property, now known as the Park-McCullough House. As a businessman, Hall was active in railroads and banking and became a director of the First National Bank of North Bennington. In a time when railroad locomotives were named like ships, the Harlem Extension Railroad, locally known as the "Corkscrew Railroad," even christened a new train the *Hiland Hall* in 1872.

Among Hall's personal interests were education (he was a supporter of the Bennington Academy), libraries and the study of the history of early Vermont. Even as a young man, he had been active in the annual commemorations of the Battle of Bennington, and this interest continued into his retirement. Hall's research and writing abilities enabled him to gain a reputation as a serious historian. He wrote numerous articles about Vermont's history and was president of the state historical society for six years. He also served as the first president of the Bennington Historical Society. His lengthy study *Early History of Vermont* (1868) is still considered a reliable source for information on the years before Vermont became a state. In his book, Hall defends the thesis that the settlers under the New Hampshire Grants were justified in their suits against the greedy claims of the Yorkers.

Hall's home for most of his life before moving into the Park-McCullough House was the Hall Farm in North Bennington. It was a charming farm complex built by his father near the center of the village. In 1818, Hall married Dolly Davis, and together, they raised six sons and two daughters. At the time of Dolly's death in 1879, the couple had been married for sixty-one years. Notable among the generations that came after him was his son-in-law Trenor Park, who distinguished himself as an attorney, inventor and entrepreneur. The husband of Hiland Hall's granddaughter Eliza, or "Lizzie," was John G. McCullough, who also served as the governor of Vermont in 1902.

In his later years, Hall became interested in the Bennington Battle Monument project and chaired the committee responsible for its "massive and lofty" design. He said that it should be "a structure that should impress the eye more by its rugged simplicity, dignity and conspicuity than by its mere elegance as a work of art." Hiland Hall died on December 18, 1885, in his ninetieth year and never lived to see the unveiling of the completed monument.

JOHN S. ROBINSON

1804–1860

The twenty-second governor of Vermont, John S. Robinson, was born in Bennington on November 10, 1804. He was a descendant of the distinguished family of Bennington's first settler, Samuel Robinson. John S. was the son of Nathan Robinson, himself the fourth son of former Vermont Governor Moses Robinson. John S. graduated in 1824 from nearby Williams College and, in 1827, was admitted to the Vermont bar.

Robinson's legal skills quickly propelled him to the forefront of his profession and suited him to the civic work he would follow. A member of the Democratic Party, he twice represented Bennington in the state's general assembly and was twice elected a member of the state senate. In 1853, he was elected governor by a joint vote of the two houses in which he had served after no candidate received a majority of the votes. He served one term as governor and was the last Democrat to be elected governor of Vermont for 110 years.

Robinson's election was spurred by political divisions stemming from the contentious issues—including slavery—of the pre–Civil War era. In the late 1840s and early 1850s, the Free Soil movement, which opposed the spread of slavery to the new territories, drained the strength of the major parties of the time. In Robinson's case, these divisions led first to his unsuccessful candidacy for the governorship as a Free Soiler in 1851 and then to a second failed bid as a Democrat in 1852. In the election of 1853, party divisions forced the legislature to choose the governor. Spurred by the enactment of Prohibition statewide, the vote finally went in Robinson's favor. Victory was

John S. Robinson. *Bennington Museum, Bennington, VT.*

brief. The following year, the consolidation of the Free Soil advocates into the new Republican Party produced a critical edge for his opponent, Stephen Royce, who then became the last Whig governor of Vermont.

As a Democrat, Robinson suffered the fate of many in minority parties. Although he was supported by his peers and associates for a number of key offices, Robinson succeeded in election to only the posts mentioned previously. In his more secure role within his own party, Robinson was made chairman of the Vermont delegation to the National Democratic Convention of 1860 on the eve of the Civil War.

Robinson died of apoplexy in Charleston, South Carolina, on April 25, 1860, while attending that same convention. His stately funeral in Bennington was attended not only by family and friends but also by a great number of his professional colleagues. Robinson's death marked the end of an era and the end of a century of prominence for the descendants of the town's early patriarch, Samuel Robinson.

WILLIAM LLOYD GARRISON

1805–1879

William Lloyd Garrison, known to most Americans today as the fierce and persistent leader of the antislavery movement, was also a journalist and opinion-maker on a far wider range of issues. In 1828, he came to Bennington to publish a short-lived weekly periodical called *Journal of the Times* before he moved on to greater fame.

Garrison was born in Newburyport, Massachusetts, in 1805. His father, a sea captain from New Brunswick, deserted the family while Garrison was still a child. His mother died before he was twenty. Apprenticed first to a shoemaker and then to a cabinetmaker, he returned to Newburyport at the age of fourteen to learn the art of printing at the local newspaper office. He soon mastered the requisite skills, becoming an invaluable assistant and learning much that his minimal public education had not supplied. Absorbing some of the spirit of the traditional press in New England, he was soon an advocate for freedom and independence. He even considered entering West Point before he decided on the career of a journalist, printer and advocate for public causes.

In 1826, Garrison initiated his first publication, the *Free Press*, in Newburyport, but its viewpoint proved too radical for his subscribers, and it failed. He then went to Boston, where he became the editor of the first American journal dedicated to temperance issues, the *National Philanthropist*, but due to a change in the paper's ownership, he stayed for less than a year.

In October 1828, when he was in his early twenties, Garrison arrived in Bennington at the invitation of supporters for the reelection of John

William Lloyd Garrison. *Bennington Museum, Bennington, VT.*

Quincy Adams. His new publication, *The Journal of the Times*, was aimed at the defeat of challenger Andrew Jackson, and his editorial position offered the young firebrand a chance to display his early concerns in favor of the abolition of slavery. Although Jackson won the election, the newspaper captured considerable support, but it lasted less than a year. In March 1829, Garrison left for Baltimore to become the coeditor of Benjamin Lundy's *Genius of Universal Emancipation*. That monthly journal focused on the gradual emancipation and recolonization of enslaved people. Such policies, however, proved too mild and conservative for Garrison. When the young editor crafted a more strident message that demanded immediate and unconditional freedom for those oppressed, Baltimore—a center of the American slave trade—responded by putting him in jail. Those who rallied to Garrison's support included the poet John Greenleaf Whittier, statesman Henry Clay and the well-known humanitarian and businessman from New York Arthur Tappan. Garrison's seven weeks in prison eventually led to the dissolution of his partnership with Lundy.

In 1831, now with a new publishing partner named Isaac Knapp, Garrison launched his best-known publication, *The Liberator*. Its subject was not limited to slavery but included articles on the issues of temperance, war and tobacco use. *The Liberator*'s radical agenda was also critical of capital punishment and imprisonment for debt. Eventually, it would encompass the principles of universal suffrage and the equality of women as well. Even in the North, some of the paper's views on these matters were considered extreme. Though Garrison sought to influence the public through moral suasion alone, he often found himself in physical danger. In one famous escapade, an Englishman named George Thompson was engaged by Garrison to speak in Boston in front of an antislavery organization. He was frightened by a mob of proslavery advocates who threatened to tar and feather him and returned home in secrecy. Garrison, attempting to fill in for the absent speaker, had to be guarded in jail overnight under police protection until it was safe for him to leave the city.

The Liberator, an extremely influential periodical during the pre–Civil War era, ceased publication after the war. Subsequently, Garrison continued his campaign for equality and dignity, garnering frequent adulation—which he often publicly resisted—in England as well as America. He died in May 1879, characteristically unsatisfied despite having witnessed great progress on much of his agenda of social reform. His stay in Bennington, to which he may have been attracted by the reputation of the noted Vermont printer and publisher Anthony Haswell, marked an early but significant step in his long career and remains an important chapter in the town's history of upholding the freedom of religious belief and freedom of the press.

CHRISTOPHER WEBBER FENTON AND DANIEL GREATBACH

1806–1865 AND ACTIVE CIRCA 1838–1861

The pottery that was first set up in the late eighteenth century by Captain John Norton had a long and illustrious history, remaining in production for over one hundred years. By 1823, John Norton had transferred ownership of the pottery to his sons Luman and Edward. The business was best known for its stoneware, especially the large crocks and jugs that are still popular with antique collectors. But the business's most celebrated periods were its years under the direction of Christopher Webber Fenton and his primary designer, Daniel Greatbach.

Christopher Webber Fenton was born in Dorset, Vermont, on January 30, 1806. As a student, he showed an early talent for drawing and design, which helped him in the East Dorset pottery that was run by his father and older brother. In 1832, Christopher married Louisa Norton and became a partner in the Nortons' Bennington pottery. Fenton was much more ambitious than the Nortons; he wanted to produce finer molded pieces rather than the wheel-thrown utilitarian stoneware favored by the Nortons. With Fenton's assistance, they became the first potters in Vermont to produce fine porcelain, china and flintware.

Fenton's productions included porcelain glazed in enamel, flint and the Rockingham style as well as Parian ware, a matte porcelain that resembles marble. Produced by molding, Parian ware was lighter and less expensive than higher-priced marble. Fenton's became the first Parian ware made in the United States. Christopher continued in the partnership with the Nortons until 1847, when he began producing delicate pieces in Bennington on his own, sometimes under the name of the U.S. Pottery Company. Then in 1858, he moved to Illinois.

The high point of Bennington's pottery probably came in 1853, when Fenton's Parian ware was exhibited at the New York Crystal Palace exhibition. A large decorative piece that now is part of the Bennington Museum's collection was created for the fair. It depicts an allegorical group, Justice and Mercy, perched on top of a tall monument. During his time in Bennington, Fenton pursued extensive experiments with new designs, glazes and colors. At the height of their success, the Fenton and Norton potteries employed some two hundred workers, contributing substantially to the economy of the town and region.

To facilitate other innovations at the pottery, a number of European potters and additional American specialists were brought to Bennington to duplicate the colors and designs sought by Americans in the best foreign and domestic work. Among these potters were Theophile Frey, a painter from the famous Sevres works in France who decorated graniteware pieces, and German pottery decorators John Hilfinger and Jacob Mertz. William Leake of Staffordshire, England, came to town to produce Parian ware, among his many other specialties. Decius Clark, a Vermont native, was a creative ceramics expert who later became yet another partner of Fenton.

The year 1852 saw the hiring of the British ceramicist Daniel Greatbach as chief designer and modeler at the pottery. His experience in English potteries gave him the skill to produce pieces comparable to the British ceramic work that was popular at the time but cost a good deal more. His notable designs included a hound-handled pitcher and other figurative pieces that he adapted for production in Bennington.

Greatbach and Fenton were responsible for some of Bennington's most remarkable ceramics, including such unusual objects as a pitcher with a Niagara Falls design and other pieces that depicted American themes, as well as an array of small animal figurines based on British counterparts. Such items were often unstamped, since buyers were known to prefer the British and European work.

Despite the success of the American Pottery Company, by 1855, it had begun to have financial difficulties. These problems were due in part to the surprisingly high price of the wood needed for firing and the cost of items broken due to shipping them over Vermont's primitive roads. By 1858, the company had closed. Greatbach left Bennington to found a new company in Georgia, and Fenton and another partner moved to Illinois. The Norton pottery remained in business here until 1894, and other potteries continued locally even beyond that date.

SETH B. HUNT

1811–1880

Seth Bliss Hunt was born in Bennington in 1811 to a family who had arrived in the community some fifteen years earlier, thirty-five years after the town's founding. His father, Jonathan, was a jeweler by trade, and at a young age, Seth began working in New York in the retail trade. His first employer was Arthur Tappan and Company. Tappan was known not only as the proprietor of the largest dry goods establishment in New York City but also as one of the leading liberals of his day and a staunch abolitionist. As a result of his own hard work and the company he kept, young Seth soon distinguished himself in the firm. He also absorbed something of the spirit of humane generosity for which Tappan and his peers were known, a quality Hunt retained throughout his life.

On reaching legal age, Hunt went into business in Manhattan with his brother Jonathan. Their shop was located on Exchange Place, a prestigious address with promising clientele. The Hunt brothers were prosperous and successful, not only serving New Yorkers but also providing merchandise for merchants from outlying regions, including southern Vermont. In this way, Hunt maintained his ties to colleagues, family and friends back home.

From 1849 to 1854, Hunt lived in Manchester, England, a manufacturing and commercial center where he made professional business ties throughout Britain and Europe. After returning to America in 1860, Seth founded a firm in Leeds, New York, for the manufacture of woolen shawls. Because of the success of this business, he built an extensive set of mill buildings on Benmont Avenue, now known as the Holden-Leonard factory, or "Big Mill,"

Stereoscopic view of Seth Hunt's Big Mill on Benmont Avenue, built in 1865. *Bennington Museum, Bennington, VT.*

to produce even more shawls. Reports of the cost of the building range from $500,000 to over $1 million. Not far away on his old family homestead, he created a stylish summer estate that he called "Maple Grove." On the lawn in front of the house, Hunt constructed a giant fountain that shot water 196 feet into the air. It was fed by fresh water from a reservoir several miles away and became a noted tourist attraction for the town. Hunt even paid for a cornet band to play once a week during the summer for the town residents. Eventually, the estate was converted into the Vermont Veterans' Home.

Because Hunt had absorbed the abolitionist views of Arthur Tappan, he aided the Free Soil Party in Kansas and was said to have done much to encourage that territory to join the Union as a free state. Hunt was also responsible for locally raising and outfitting regiments to fight in the Civil War.

As a philanthropist, he supported a number of churches and educational institutions. In 1865, he and North Bennington's Trenor Park undertook the mission to provide Bennington with its Free Library building. Located at the corner of Main and Silver Streets, it has served many generations of Benningtonians as an institution for free education and culture.

Seth Hunt died on April 20, 1880, while at his New York residence on Nineteenth Street. Upon Seth's death, Bennington mourned the loss of not only his commercial leadership but also his concern for the community, especially those in need. He was singular in putting his own gains to use for others, and public expressions of grief were uniform in their praise of his generosity.

HENRY E. BRADFORD

1819–1878

Henry Bradford, the founder of the prosperous H.E. Bradford Company knitting mills on East Main Street, was born in Southbridge, Massachusetts, in 1819. He came to Bennington in 1854, having spent several years in the manufacture of woolens at North Amherst and Millbury in his native state. In Bennington, Bradford continued to manufacture cloth, but he later turned his attention to the production of hosiery. Bradford's obituary described him as a staunch Republican, a Mason and a Methodist.

In 1858, Bradford's mill was significant, as it was the last of Bennington's wool mills to be converted to knit cotton, a business that proved to be a sustaining one for the town despite numerous fires and setbacks.

Bradford's mills were also remembered as the scene of one of the town's worst disasters. On January 20, 1874, his mills were the site of a massive explosion and fire, apparently caused by a defective gasoline pipe. As with other modern advances of its day, the benefits of the "patent underground gas works" installed at the Bradford mill to provide lighting were thought to outweigh their dangers. A leaky pipe, however, allowed a huge quantity of gas fumes to accumulate in the lower portions of mills. When an unsuspecting employee struck a match, it touched off a blast whose force was felt throughout the village.

A *Bennington Banner* "extra" put out at 1:00 a.m. the next day described the event in detail. Nine were listed as having been killed, with seven listed as injured. The bodies were still being removed from the site as the newspaper went to press. The Bradford house directly across Main Street from the mill was used as a temporary morgue. One fatality, Laura Vaughn, was the widow of a sergeant who had been killed at the Battle of Gettysburg. She left behind her mother and a young daughter who had been dependent on her for support. Another, Elizabeth Cunningham, was the widow of a man who had been killed in an earlier industrial explosion at a Bennington gunpowder mill. She left seven children under sixteen years of age. Four of the victims were young single women who were still in their teens—in one case, a remaining sister was badly injured as well.

Henry E. Bradford. *Bennington Museum, Bennington, VT.*

While technological advances have always been attractive to Americans, incidents such as the Bradford mill explosion, with its tragic effects on families and the community, helped lead to reforms in safety and labor laws. Inventions like the gas lighting system employed in the mill were soon under far stricter control and, in some cases, outlawed altogether. The mill itself, on the other hand, was soon rebuilt and once again produced the knitted goods for which it was known. As the *Banner* reported, the mill was soon reopened, and "the hum and buzz of the rapidly moving machinery could be heard quite a distance away." By the late 1800s, the Bradford mills employed about 250 workers and turned out twenty-five thousand undershirts a year. The business continued after Henry's death in April 1878 under the guidance of his sons and grandson until finally closing for good on January 31, 1961.

TRENOR PARK

1823–1882

The story of Trenor Park, a Bennington attorney, entrepreneur, businessman and builder of the splendid Victorian Park-McCullough House in North Bennington, is one of the persistence, achievement and imagination characteristic of Americans in the mid-nineteenth century. It is also a reminder of the opportunities produced by the immense changes at that time, to which ambitious individuals like Park responded.

Trenor W. Park was born in Woodford on December 8, 1823, to Luther and Cynthia Park. He was the fourth of eight children. Though his family was poor, his parents provided a home that taught strong moral values. At an early age, Park began to plan for the betterment of both himself and his family. He began the study of law at sixteen with a prominent Bennington attorney, Alanson Lyman, and was admitted to the Vermont bar as soon as he was eligible at the age of twenty-one. Shortly after that, in 1846, he married Laura V.S. Hall, the daughter of eminent attorney and public servant Hiland Hall and his wife, the former Dolly Tuttle Davis. Trenor and Laura Park eventually had three children.

The entry of California into the Union played a key role in the good fortune of Park and his extended family. When Park's father-in-law, Hiland Hall, was appointed federal land commissioner of California in 1851 to help settle the complex land claims of the new state, Trenor and Laura joined him in San Francisco. First joining the prestigious law firm of Halleck, Peachy and Billings, where he quickly became a partner, Park soon set up his own office. One of his principal clients was the soldier, explorer and presidential aspirant John C. Fremont, whose Mariposa estate east of San Francisco was in the center of gold country.

Through the management of the affairs and finances of Fremont and other wealthy Californians, Park obtained oversight and eventually ownership interest in important properties and businesses, ultimately amassing a huge fortune. When he returned east in 1863, he used these assets to increase the range and productivity of his industrial holdings. Among his endeavors were the founding and expansion of railroads and mines, including the Vermont Central, Western Vermont and Lebanon Springs Railroads, and his partnership in the Emma Silver Mine, one of the best-known mining swindles of its time. His investments were varied; he established the First National Bank of North Bennington and, through control of its railroad, played an important role in the development of the Panama Canal.

On their return east, the Parks took up an extravagant life far removed from the one they had left behind in Bennington some ten years earlier. Still, they didn't entirely separate themselves from the friends and social roots they previously shared. Next to the comfortable old farmhouse where Hiland Hall lived, they built an immense thirty-five-room "country house" in the Second Empire style, with touches of the Italianate Romantic Revival popular at the time. For the next one hundred years, the house served as the family's getaway during summers and holidays. Their winters were spent in New York City in equal, although more urban, comfort. In addition to their own business concerns, the Parks and their descendants remained involved in the Bennington community. The Free Library in Bennington, given to the town by Park and a contemporary, the industrialist Seth Hunt, was only one of a number of gifts the town received from this generous family. Park was a major contributor to New York's Fresh Air Fund and a donor and trustee of the University of Vermont.

Trenor Park. *Bennington Museum, Bennington, VT.*

From his youth until his death, Park was aggressive and often controversial. In San Francisco, he had been associated with the *San Francisco Bulletin*, whose editor was later assassinated. Park was also the attorney for the city's notorious Vigilance Committee, which often took the law into their own hands. His business practices, while effective, left a legacy of contentiousness as well as accomplishment. In the celebrated case of a silver mine in the Far West, which proved less valuable than the price he had brokered it for, the faint praise he received from the seller was perhaps little better than the damnation he received from the buyer. Benningtonians, however, continue to see Park as a hero who went west to make his fortune and, unlike many others, succeeded.

Park died aboard the ship *San Blas* while en route to Panama on December 13, 1882. He had recently married Ella Nichols of San Francisco following the death of his first wife, Laura. The house of his widow, like the Park-McCullough House, has been incorporated into a charming public park in San Rafael, California, a short distance north of her native city. Trenor's body was brought back and buried in New York's Greenwood Cemetery, but it was later transferred to the Old Bennington Cemetery.

HENRY W. PUTNAM SR. AND HENRY W. PUTNAM JR.

1825–1915 AND 1864–1938

Henry W. Putnam Sr., one of the town's great industrialists and the builder of the fine Putnam Hotel at the center of town on the corner of Main and South Streets, was a good example of the philanthropic nature of so many Bennington residents. He was a typical self-made man who profited from the country's prosperity at the turn of the twentieth century. He and his son also became the principal founders of the Putnam Hospital, which is now called the Southwestern Vermont Medical Center.

In addition to the seventy-five-room hotel that Putnam built between 1870 and 1872 to give the town much-needed lodgings for businessmen and tourists, he was also responsible for the construction of Bennington's Opera House, which once stood on the opposite corner. Built in 1892, the large, towered Victorian building continued to function as a theater and shopping complex until it burned down in 1959. These establishments reinforced the town's reputation as a cultural and commercial center and gave locals and visitors facilities superior to any others in the region.

Henry Putnam Sr. was born in 1825 in the small hamlet of Boquet, part of the town of Essex in New York State on the western shores of Lake Champlain. His parents had been early pioneers in that area. Henry's father, Hiram Putnam, originally worked as a farmer but got into other investments, including a sawmill, an iron foundry and a general store. His son would follow his example with the ownership of several industrial ventures.

In 1848, when he was still in his early twenties, Henry Sr. set out to make his mark in California. He was apparently not drawn by gold fever, since the

Bust of Henry Putnam Sr. at the Southern Vermont Medical Center. *Photograph by Bill Morgan.*

discovery of gold at Sutter's Mill was still a year away, but he found that he was in the right place at the right time. As the gold rush boomed, the enterprising Henry did not take up the pick and shovel as other prospectors did; instead, he found a niche for himself by supplying water to the residents of San Francisco, a profitable business he would invest in throughout his life. Using a horse and wagon, he sold fresh water in corked bottles for three to five dollars a month. He soon made his first substantial fortune in that manner. His business also presented him with his first technical problem: how to keep the corks in the bottles as his cart jostled along on the unpaved roads. This he solved by acquiring patents for various types of bottle stoppers, which led to his second fortune.

On his return to Boquet from California, Putnam stayed in his hometown long enough to marry Irene Crossman, and he set up a successful business operating some mills and a factory. After moving to Cleveland, he invested heavily in Ohio real estate. Irene died soon after their marriage, and in 1862, Henry married the widow of an eminent Cleveland physician, Dr. Henry Everett. It turned out that Mary Hamlin Everett Putnam had family roots in western Massachusetts, not far from Bennington, and her twin sister was married to a member of Bennington's Dewey family. Through her previous marriage, Mary had a son named Edward H. Everett, who would later become one of Bennington's wealthiest summer residents and build the huge mansion that still stands on the side of Mount Anthony. Though drawn to New York City for business reasons, the Putnam family spent most of their summers between 1864 and 1898 in Bennington. At that point, Henry moved permanently to San Diego, California, for his health.

In New York City, Henry Sr. was involved in numerous enterprises, including a hardware business and the Brooklyn Elevated Railway, part of the city's subway system. Industrious and generous, even on his "vacations" in Bennington, Putnam became a major benefactor of the town. He bought the mills previously owned by Olin Scott on North Street near the bridge over the Walloomsac, and there, he began manufacturing his patented "Lightning" jars, which employed a specially twisted wire that held the caps on the glass bottles securely. His other products included washing machine wringers, double-pointed carpet tacks, fruit jar tops and machines for making barbed wire. Directly across the river, he built a fine mansion that was torn down; the site is now the parking lot of a drugstore.

In 1885–86, Putnam also laid out a water system for Bennington that provided the entire town with safe, pure drinking water. Demonstrating his public spirit, Henry Sr. gave the water system to the town of Bennington in 1912 with the understanding that the profits from the sale of water would go to maintaining a hospital for the community, a measure that improved the health as well as convenience for those it served. Putnam did not live to see the completion of the hospital building, but his son, Henry Putnam Jr., carried on the work and named it in his honor.

Henry Jr. was Henry Sr.'s only son with Mary. Henry Jr. grew up to be as private as his father was public and magnanimous. Living a wealthy bachelor's life devoted to yachts and vacation homes, Henry Jr. spent far less time in Bennington than his parents had, although he retained ownership of the Putnam House Hotel until 1923. When his father died in 1915, Henry Jr. stepped forward to offer the $90,000 necessary to complete his father's hospital project. For the rest of his life, Henry Jr. continued to support the hospital while he still managed to live a comfortable personal life. By the time of his own death in 1938, Henry Jr. had contributed far more than his original gift, including a bequest of $3 million toward the hospital's endowment fund.

The Putnam tradition lives on in the names of many buildings and services throughout Bennington and the region. The hotel and medical center alone stand as highly visible reminders of the generous family.

HENRY SQUIRES

1825–1907

In the early 1800s, a man named Buckley Squires arrived in Bennington and immediately went into business, establishing two sawmills for hemlock and spruce, a factory for making chairs and a tannery. He married one of the potter John Norton's girls, Lucretia, and raised a large family of at least ten children with her. Remarkably, one of their sons, Henry Squires, was destined to find greatness beyond Bennington and became one of the world's most famous opera singers during the Victorian era.

Henry was born in Bennington on May 7, 1825, and as he grew up, he was put to work in his father's tannery. People described him as a ruddy, robust-looking young man who liked to sing as he worked. One woman reminisced that "the first and greatest ecstatic enjoyment music ever gave me was to hear that young man sing." In the days before radio and television advertising, political candidates often had songs written for their campaigns. Henry Buckley was remembered locally for his rendition of a song he sang at rallies for William Henry Harrison's 1840 presidential campaign. It went: "For Tippecanoe and Tyler, too. / And with them we'll beat little Van, Van, Van. / Van is a used up man. / And with them we'll beat little Van." Maybe the lyrics weren't great, but the tune was memorable.

Four years later, in 1844, the campaign song for Henry Clay was presented at the area's Whig convention by The Vermont Minstrels, Mr. Whitney and Henry Squires. Squires caused a sensation, even if Clay did not win the election. This exposure to public performance inspired young Squires to seriously study music in Boston, and by 1847, the newspapers

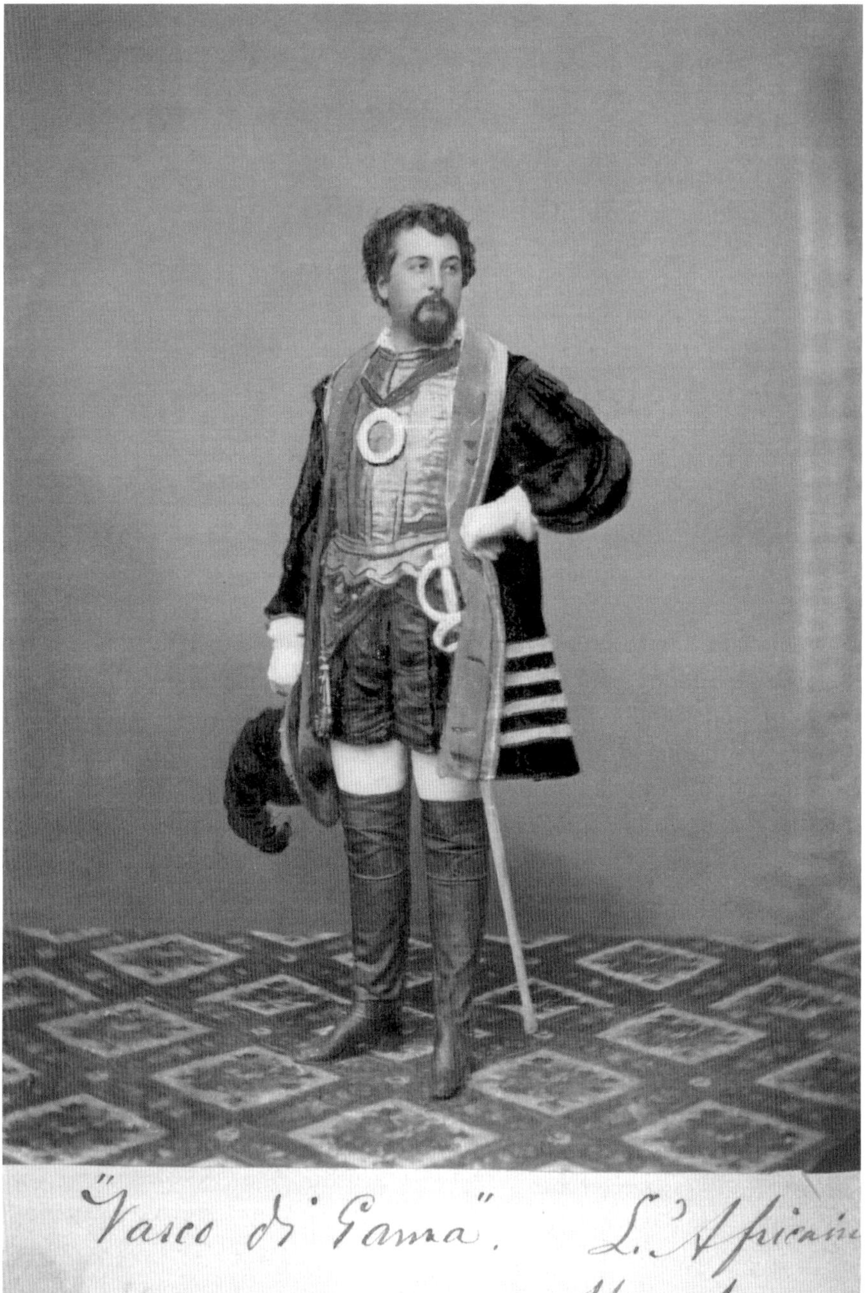

Henry Squires in the role of Vasco di Gama, 1860s. *Bennington Museum, Bennington, VT.*

were reporting that he was giving concerts in Bangor and other cities along the eastern coast of New England with "flattering success." He returned to Troy to study further with George William Warren, and at one performance at St. Paul's Church in Albany, he met Lucy Eastcott. The two singers toured as part of a quartet before Henry made his first solo appearance in New York City in 1851 singing at Niblo's Theater, one of the grandest auditoriums in the city. By then, he had progressed from campaign songs and church hymns to operas such as *Fra Diavolo* and Rossini's *Stabat Mater*. Soon, he was being called the "Great American Tenor" by music critics and newspaper reporters.

In 1852, he left America for additional study in Italy. In Naples, he took lessons from Michele Ruta, the great Italian classical composer. Maybe not by coincidence, Lucy Eastcott was also in Naples, and although she was married at the time, she and Squires became companions. Squires easily won the hearts of his Italian audiences and toured the country to great acclaim. Following Mrs. Eastcott (now changed to Escott) to England in 1857, Squires sang in a troupe that she had organized under the new name Lucy Escott Opera Company. The following year, the couple returned to America, giving concerts everywhere they went, including Albany. There, the local papers commented that Squires's classical singing was enjoyable, but the local audiences still liked his ballads best. For the next year, Squires toured the country, arriving in California at the end of 1860. There, he reunited once more with Mrs. Escott. Her entire opera company boarded a ship there, and for the next eight years, they performed to sold-out crowds all over Australia. This was to be their biggest triumph, and Squires was hailed as one of the greatest grand opera tenors of his day.

By late 1869, Squires was back in Vermont, where the press said he enjoyed "considerable celebrity." On June 21, 1870, Squires married Lucy Escott, although no record of a divorce from her first husband has been found. The couple's short stay here was followed by a trip to Paris, where they lived until Lucy's death in 1895. After that, Henry returned to Bennington and lived here during the summers. He suffered a fatal stroke and died on January 13, 1907, at the age of eighty-two while visiting his brother in Iowa. His body was brought back to Bennington, and a funeral was held for him in St. Peter's Episcopal Church. He was buried next to his wife, Lucy, in the Old Bennington Cemetery.

OLIN SCOTT

1832–1913

One of Bennington's most successful industrialists of the nineteenth century was Olin Scott. In his mills on the east end of Pleasant Street, he fabricated machinery that was used throughout the world. His generosity in civic and educational affairs is still recognized and felt by the community today, and he is remembered as not just an inventor and manufacturer but also one of the town's great philanthropists.

Olin Scott was born in Bennington on February 27, 1832, to a family descended from such early settlers as the Fays, Saffords and Sages, all of whom made their mark on the town. With only the most basic instruction from the local schools, Scott developed a pattern of diligence, enterprise and self-education that set him apart from most of his peers.

When Scott was just eleven, his father found him a job in a retail store in Troy. A year and a half later, he took a similar job as a clerk in a store in Albany. At fourteen, he returned to Bennington so he could spend a year studying at the old Union Academy while he worked for his room and board. Following his brief formal education, he served as an apprentice for three years, learning the trade of a millwright with Truman Olin, his mother's brother. Through that practical experience, he learned the art of designing, building and setting up mills. Eager to learn, he also studied engineering and mathematics and eventually was able to attend the North Bennington Academy for one more year of schooling.

In 1855, he turned to millwork as a young professional and worked in several locations in New England. Within a year or two, he became the

Olin Scott. *Bennington Museum, Bennington, VT.*

foreman of Grover & Harrington in Bennington until it went out of business in 1857. He soon became the foreman of the Eagle Iron Foundry and Machine Shops, which operated in buildings near the North Street bridge, some of which are still standing. In 1858, he entered a partnership with the mill's owner, Lemuel Grover, and Olin took charge of the Bennington Machine Works. Five years later, at the height of the Civil War, he bought out Grover's share in the machine shop, and the following year, he purchased the entire foundry. By then, he was only thirty-two years old and a prosperous mill owner and manufacturer in his own right, poised for further success.

The specialty of Scott's mills became the production of the machines employed in the manufacture of gunpowder. In fact, much of the powder used by the Union army during the war was processed through the equipment he made here. To be clear, he didn't make gunpowder, but he made the machines that made gunpowder. In 1865, he consolidated his mills into a single factory complex on upper Pleasant Street and sold the old North Street buildings to Henry W. Putnam. For the rest of his life, Scott focused on his operations there, even building his own spectacular Stick-style house next to the factory.

An entrepreneur at heart, Olin expanded the business, and in 1869, he built similar mills in Michigan, New York, Ohio and Pennsylvania. He ran these businesses until 1887, at which point he sold them all and turned his attention to consulting for several firms in the powder business, including the giant DuPont Company of Delaware. Later, Scott began to manufacture machinery used to make wood pulp and paper. Expanding his investments even further, in 1892, he became president of the Lasher Stocking Company, a Bennington firm that made men's hosiery.

Scott married Celeste Gilbert in 1856, but although they hoped for a large family, the couple had no children who outlived them. Olin was a long-standing member of the Second Congregational Church and belonged to a number of civic organizations. During the Civil War, Scott had been exempted from service in the military due to the importance of

Olin Scott's home on Pleasant Street still stands. *Bennington Museum, Bennington, VT.*

his businesses, but he later held a commission in the Vermont National Guard and is often referred to as Colonel Scott as a result. His interest in the town's history led him to become one of the early supporters of the plan to build a monument to commemorate the Battle of Bennington. In addition, he provided most of the funds for the Seth Warner statue that was placed at the top of Monument Avenue to honor the Patriot leader. Then he fabricated the monument's iron stairway, which became an important tourist attraction. He even donated toward the construction of the town's Masonic temple, which still stands on Main Street. He served as Bennington's auditor for many years and did much to support education. He established a scholarship fund in his name, which still provides training and education for young students, something that had been so important to Scott himself.

While determination and hard work did much to bring success to Scott, his achievements also owe something to the times in which he lived. The role his machines played during the Civil War and other nineteenth-century conflicts assured a profitable basis for his business and made Bennington's importance even greater. No one doubts that the true success of his business, however, was based on Scott's own merits. As one commentator wrote in a 1914 book about the Scott factory, "They have small fear of competition as they take particular pains to make a superior machine that others find difficult to duplicate."

Olin Scott died in Bennington in 1913, honored as one of Bennington's most important self-made citizens. At the time of his death, his businesses were valued at over $2 million, a substantial sum in those days.

ALEXANDER DRYSDALE

1832–1884

Drysdale's department store, a fixture for many years in downtown Bennington, was founded in 1873 by local entrepreneur Alexander Drysdale. Incorporating a wide variety of products for household and family life, department stores represented a new development in many American towns during the 1900s. In a single visit, shoppers might examine curtains, furniture, rugs or clothes or buy the material to make them themselves. In their effort to collect and present a diversity of goods reflecting the popular tastes of the time, department stores represented a new opportunity for those in rural areas, like Bennington, to live in a style more like that of their urban peers.

Drysdale was an engineer by trade who originally came to Bennington from Scotland to help his brother William set up the looms in the newly constructed Big Mill. But by 1873, he found himself manager of the company store on the corner of Benmont Avenue and River Street. Leaving the mill's employ, Alexander went into business for himself and set up his own store farther east on River Street near North Street. It was his son who, in 1891, made the next move to an even larger building that still stands on the corner of North and River Streets. After the business moved again in 1906—its final move—it became an important commercial anchor on South Street. The large building is known as the Park Block and was strategically located next to the county courthouse. That building with a modified storefront on the street level still survives today and has been recently renovated.

Interior of Drysdale's Department Store in 1905. *Bennington Museum, Bennington, VT.*

As late as the mid-twentieth century, Drysdale's, like Adams Hardware on Main Street and the nearby Burt Brothers clothing store, was still arranged and fitted out in the nineteenth-century manner. In all three locations, shelving and counters were made of wood. At both Drysdale's and Adams, the store managers seated themselves at a desk suspended on a mezzanine between the ground floor and upper levels. From this perch, they could work while unobtrusively observing all the activities in the store. For shoppers of a literary inclination, the scene of the owner in spectacles quietly perusing his accounting books while keeping a keen eye on employees and customers alike should bring Charles Dickens to mind. After Alexander Drysdale died in 1884, the business remained in the family and was managed by his son Robert (1862–1920) under the name A. Drysdale and Son. Later, the next generation of Drysdales continued this local retail tradition with Alexander Best Robert Drysdale (1904–1984).

The family's interest in the town is reflected by not only their retail efforts but also the 1927 publication of Alexander B.R. Drysdale's small volume titled *Bennington's Book*. It was written at the time of the sesquicentennial of the Battle of Bennington and contains a brief history of Bennington. It contains commentary on the town's two previous celebrations, the centennial of the battle in 1877 and the dedication of the monument and celebration of statehood in 1891. In a volume meant primarily as a memento, Drysdale asks rhetorically: Why was this book written? His answer: Simply to satisfy himself concerning the legends of history he had heard about his native town.

Like a number of the stores that defined downtown Bennington, Drysdale's was met with stiff competition from the influx of larger chain stores and shopping centers that came in the 1950s. The store eventually closed in 1977 after more than one hundred years in business.

RICHARD HENRY GREEN

1833–1877

In the year 1857, the first Black student graduated from Yale University; his name was Richard Henry Green. Born in New Haven, Connecticut, he was raised only a few blocks from the Yale campus. His father was a boot maker and a very religious man who helped organize St. Luke's Episcopal Church for the Black community in New Haven. After college, Green came to live in Bennington and Hoosick, New York, for much of his short life and was buried in the Old Bennington Cemetery.

Green was born in 1853, and at the age of twenty, he entered Yale, listed as "mulatto." Four years later, in 1857, he graduated with his degree. Initially, he worked as a teacher, first in Milford, Connecticut, and then later in Bennington at the Bennington Seminary. The seminary had been established by James Ballard in 1829 on Seminary Lane after Ballard was fired from his position at the brick Bennington Academy up the hill on Monument Avenue. In March 1860, Green began to study medicine with a local Bennington doctor named Benjamin F. Morgan. Green taught at the seminary for only a few years before he decided to formally enroll at Dartmouth College in late 1863 to pursue a career in medicine. He earned his medical degree from Dartmouth with the class of 1864, but by that time, he had already enrolled in the navy as an acting assistant surgeon.

In the navy during the Civil War, he was posted to the USS *State of Georgia* for about a year while the ship blockaded the North Carolina coast. While awaiting orders for his next ship, Richard had a few months off, and in September 1864, he married a woman he had met in Bennington named

Charlotte "Lottie" Caldwell. Green was then assigned duty on the steamer USS *Seneca*, which patrolled the Cape Fear River area for the remainder of the war.

Richard Green. *Bennington Museum, Bennington, VT.*

After the war, Green and his family settled first in Cambridge and then in Hoosick, where it appears he changed the spelling of his name to "Greene." He established his practice in Rensselaer County and appears to have been very popular with his patients. When it came time to enroll in the 1870 census, he was listed as "white." Whether that was his choice or the census-taker's is unknown. Richard Henry Greene's life as a country doctor was cut short on March 23, 1877, when he died of heart disease at the age of forty-three. He left behind his wife and seven-year-old daughter. He was remembered as a man who was "fond of the study of natural history and spent much time collecting plants and objects of interest in that department. He was a most amiable and genial man, and a practical Christian."

JOHN G. McCULLOUGH

1835–1915

John Griffith McCullough, the forty-ninth governor of Vermont, was born in Newark, Delaware, on September 16, 1835. At the age of twenty, he graduated with honors from Delaware College and then received his degree in law from the University of Pennsylvania in 1858. John stayed in Philadelphia to practice law, but for health reasons, he soon moved to California, first to the town of Mariposa and then to San Francisco. There, he achieved considerable success. The prosperity brought on by the gold rush offered him opportunities for achievement in the profession of law. Through his skill in business, he expanded his interests into other areas, especially politics. He represented Mariposa in the state legislature in 1861, served as a state senator in 1863 and was California's attorney general from 1863 to 1867.

While in California, McCullough met Benningtonian Trenor W. Park, who was living there with his family. Both John and Trenor shared interests in politics, business and law in Mariposa and San Francisco. His relationship with Park was strengthened considerably in 1871, when he married Park's daughter, Eliza Hall Park. The couple returned to Vermont in 1873. Here, John immersed himself in commerce and finance, often working with his father-in-law on matters of business. From 1873 to 1883, he was vice president of the Panama Railway under the direction of the railroad's president, Trenor Park. In the decade following Park's death in 1882, McCullough became one of the leaders in the reorganization of the Erie Railroad, and in later years, from 1900 to 1910, he was the president of the Chicago and Erie Railroad.

John G. McCullough. *Bennington Museum, Bennington, VT.*

He also became the president of both the Bennington and Rutland Railway and the North Bennington National Bank. He was a director of numerous other railroads and corporations, including the Bank of New York; the American Fidelity Company; the Atchison, Topeka and Santa Fe Railroad Company; and the Lackawanna Steel Company.

In Vermont, McCullough maintained his interest in politics and served as a state senator from Bennington County from 1898 to 1900. During this time, he was also elected president pro tempore of the senate. He represented Vermont several times at Republican National Conventions before he became the governor of the state from 1902 to 1904.

In John McCullough, the Park family found the perfect partner for their activities in both business and philanthropic affairs. John and Eliza, or "Lizzie," as she was better known, took over the management of the immense Park-McCullough House in North Bennington. After Trenor Park's death, the McCulloughs purchased the remaining shares of the house from Lizzie's siblings. By spending each summer in Vermont, the McCulloughs helped forge a pattern that made Bennington a highly popular location as the vacation destination of the wealthy. The Park-McCullough House was only the first of what became many estates and fine homes in the area. The philanthropy of the family toward local institutions also became a model for others.

John G. McCullough died on May 29, 1915, at the age of seventy-nine. His wife continued to oversee the management of the house and the affairs of their family until her death in 1938. She and John were buried in the family mausoleum in the Old Bennington Cemetery. Lizzie's small volume of memoirs, *Within One's Memory*, offers a charming view into her life, including her early adventures as a child in Mariposa and nearby Yosemite during the post–gold rush period.

HENRY THEODORE CUSHMAN

1844–1922

For nearly a century, the H.T. Cushman Manufacturing Company of North Bennington was one of the town's most well-known industries. Founded in 1886, it began making wooden accessories before it branched off into traditional-style "colonial" furniture that found a market throughout the country. Until recent years, it produced sturdy products that continue to be in strong demand and are still popular with families and collectors today.

The founder of the company, Henry Theodore Cushman, was born in Bennington in 1844 to a family with strong ties to the town and the region. His great-grandfather Charles Cushman had been a leader in early Bennington, serving in the Revolution before assuming various civic and religious positions in the community. The family also descended from Robert Cushman, who arrived with the Pilgrims on the *Mayflower*.

Cushman was educated in Bennington, but in 1860, when Henry was still a teenager, his father died, forcing him to take over the family business to support his widowed mother and his two sisters. His father, John Cushman, had owned a hat and clothing store on Main Street near the Franklin House Hotel. When the Civil War broke out, Cushman enlisted in the Union army, even though he was technically too young to serve. The army found that his organizational abilities deriving from his business experience made him very useful. Henry was said to have been the youngest quartermaster in the army, but despite his youth, he was highly commended for his service. A letter from General Lewis A. Grant attests that Cushman volunteered for

Advertisement with John Cushman using his shoe shining machine. *Bennington Museum, Bennington, VT.*

dangerous duties during the Battle of the Wilderness, as well as several other battles around Spotsylvania. He was "not only an excellent quartermaster, but a brave and gallant soldier," wrote the general. At one point during the war, Cushman was in charge of a small detail of about thirty men when they ran into the famous Confederate guerrilla Colonel John Singleton Mosby. Cushman and his men skirmished with Mosby briefly before they managed to get away. After the war, Cushman and Mosby struck up a friendly correspondence that lasted for several years.

Following the war, Cushman returned to Bennington and engaged in the manufacture of stationers' goods. In 1867, he married Eliza Davis Hall, the granddaughter of a former governor, Hiland Hall. He soon turned to the manufacture of furniture, which proved to be the main product for which his company is still known. For many years, the Cushman Company was one of the largest and steadiest employers in the area. Its trademark "Colonial Creations" are still found in use in many homes and businesses, and they are collected by aficionados as well.

By 1877, Cushman's business was secure enough to enable him to serve on the planning committee of the centennial celebration for the Battle of Bennington. He later was on the committee that built the Bennington Battle Monument and also enjoyed membership in other civic and military organizations. For many years, he was president of the village of North Bennington.

Cushman's, as the stone factory on River Street in North Bennington was known locally, was a good example of a thoroughly regional industry. With timber available nearby, the factory, with its sawmill and finishing equipment—band saws, planers, drills and lathes—used local labor to turn these natural resources into products that had a large market outside the area. The result was both a steady flow of income into the region and employment for many. Today, the buildings still stand but have been converted to the manufacture of other products. Cushman died in 1922 and was buried in Bennington's Village Cemetery. His business was run by his descendants until 1964, when it was sold to Green Mountain Furniture.

NORMAN PUFFER

1847–1912

The story of Norman Puffer, while unique in the town's history, is one of a number of such narrative accounts that links Bennington to events of importance on a national and international scale. Born in Bennington in 1847, Puffer was only fourteen in June 1861, when he enlisted in the Second Vermont Regiment as one of the first Vermonters to volunteer for the Civil War. There is always uncertainty when it comes to identifying the youngest or oldest soldier in any war, but if Norman was not the youngest from Vermont, he was at least the second youngest. Recently, another soldier has been identified who may have been a few days younger than Puffer. Norman became the drummer boy, first for the Second Vermont Infantry Band and later for the Tenth Vermont Infantry. He served for the duration of the war, and when peace came, he had not yet turned eighteen. His older brothers, Wales and Alfred Puffer, also served in the Union army.

Puffer was always one to enjoy telling a good story, and because he entered the army so young, he could have been around for many of the important events of that war. He said he was at the surrender of General Robert E. Lee at Appomattox and that he participated in the triumphal review of troops in Washington that followed. According to his later description, published in the *Banner* in 1909, Washington, D.C., in early April 1865, was a city bathed in the glow of victory and the jubilance of relief. Soldiers roamed the streets cheering at the latest dispatches, and everywhere, patriotic decorations accentuated the festive mood. He remembered a torchlight procession through the grounds of the White House and the beaming look of President

Norman Puffer. *Bennington Museum, Bennington, VT.*

Lincoln as Puffer passed before him among the troops in review. Granting him the enthusiasm and motivation it would take for a young boy to survive a harrowing war, we can understand the distress he must have felt a few days later when he found himself an eyewitness to the assassination of his revered commander-in-chief President Lincoln.

As a young soldier still in his teens, Puffer noted with interest newspaper reports from April 14 that announced Lincoln was planning to attend Ford's Theatre that evening to see the actress Laura Keene in the celebrated comedy *Our American Cousin*. Obtaining a midnight pass from his commander, Puffer secured a ticket to the theater. Pushing through the throngs that were waiting for standing room, he seated himself toward the back of the hall. The presidential party arrived around 9:00 p.m. After considerable applause, the play resumed. Sometime later, Puffer recounted the sound of a pistol shot. He thought it odd, as nothing in the drama required it. The actors on the stage also looked about, confused as to its cause. The house became quiet. A moment later, John Wilkes Booth, himself an actor, jumped to the stage.

"When I first saw Booth," recounted Puffer, "he was on the stage on one knee. He rose slowly and faced the audience, then turned and walked from the stage with a limp that indicated that he was badly hurt, passing out through the side wings. He carried something in his hand that might have been a knife or pistol. His face was as pale as death; the actors stood aside to let him pass."

Suddenly, a man in the dress circle above shouted out that the president had been shot. Pandemonium let loose. Women screamed and fainted; there was a great jostling, and many were trampled and hurt. Puffer remembered a man standing on a table or chair on the stage gesticulating and shouting at the top of his lungs, but he could not be heard. Soon, Miss Keene came to the front of the stage to calm the audience and request them to disperse as quickly as possible. Puffer soon returned to the street.

The crowds who roamed the streets that night were of a different mood than those who had prevailed in jubilance before. Rumors were abroad, and uncertainty prevailed. Secretary of State William Seward had also been attacked. Eventually, Puffer returned to camp to tell his comrades his unhappy tale.

After the war, Puffer returned to Bennington and went to work for Alonzo Valentine in his knitting mill. Around 1880, with the skills he had learned at the Valentine mills, Puffer helped organize the Bennington Knitting Company, which became a leading manufacturer of ladies' and children's underwear. Later, he was connected with the Bennington Wax Paper Company as vice president and became a director of the Bennington County National Bank. He was a member of many civic and veterans' groups and served as a village trustee and village president. In many ways, he was representative of his generation and his time. He died in 1912, having consigned his reminiscence of April 14, 1865, to the *Banner* some three years earlier.

It is an interesting side note that Lincoln had planned to spend his summer vacation of 1865 at the Equinox House in Manchester. Though these plans, of course, never came to be, his son Robert Todd Lincoln eventually returned to build Hildene, the beautiful country mansion in Manchester that Vermonters and many others continue to enjoy today.

HAWLEY C. WHITE

1848–1925

It is a little-known fact that North Bennington was once home to one of the largest photographic companies in the world, making stereoscopes and stereographs as well as the Radioptican, a precursor to the picture projector. Later, as the demand for stereoscopic views waned, the company branched off to produce one of the country's most popular toys, the Kiddie Kar. Founded in New York City in 1870, the H.C. White Company came to North Bennington in 1874 at the height of the late nineteenth century's popular boom in photography.

The company advertised directly to parents and promised "to make home entertainments more alluring than those offered outside, in which the older members of the family often have no share, and which range all the way from innocently amusing to the really harmful. What father has not watched the growing impatience of his favorite son for those town and city diversions that can only result in harm; staying awake of nights to await his son's late arrival, racking his brains for some way in which to provide the necessary recreation and amusement of his children that will not make them look upon him as a hated enemy and joy-killer?" Their products were marketed as a solution to keep kids at home.

Establishing a large factory along Paran Creek near the confluence with the Walloomsac River, Hawley C. White and, later, his children, Hawley Jr. and Clarence, soon became primary producers of stereographic photographs, stereoscopic viewers and other photographic equipment. Unfortunately, the original factory that had been built by the Burden Iron Works burned to the

Employees sorting stereo cards inside the H.C. White Company factory, circa 1905. *Bennington Museum, Bennington, VT.*

ground in 1881, but it was quickly rebuilt by White and enlarged to contain more than fifty thousand square feet.

By the early 1900s, well after the H.C. White Company's establishment, surviving photographs show it as a large wooden factory in the area known as Hinsdillville, named after its early settlers. A large span of glass at one end is the telltale sign of a photographic studio, perhaps that of Clarence White, one of several family members who served as photographers for the firm. By 1922, those buildings had been replaced by the brick structures that remain on the site.

In the heyday of the stereograph, large firms like H.C. White also contracted to buy and reprint the negatives of other photographers and publishers, giving them a larger range of subject matter. Negatives produced by the White Company are sometimes found under the labels of other firms, and some of the large numbers of pictures seen on the Whites' stereos are clearly the work of European and other independent photographers.

The stereograph was a double photographic print that, when viewed through a special viewer called a stereoscope, gives a three-dimensional illusion. The effect these had on social and artistic life was akin to the arrival of the television, and the products became ubiquitous across America.

With the decline in interest in the stereopticon, the H.C. White Company had to find other products to replace it. One of these was the popular Kiddie Kar, which came to be its best-known product for children. Clarence White originally invented it in 1915 as an amusement for one of the White children, but by 1919, an article in the trade magazine *Hardware Age* had reported that 1.25 million Kiddie Kars were being manufactured each year. They were made of local materials, maple for the wheels, boxwood for the seats, yellow birch for the bolsters and white pine for the handles. The feature that sold the product was its simple, sturdy design that was intended to hold up to the roughest treatment any youngster could dole out, and it was sold for only two dollars.

Hawley White was also known around town for his early interest in the automobile. As early as 1907, he was the Vermont representative for the Peerless Motor Company. Hawley died in 1925, but his company survived for another decade. It closed for good in 1935 in large part due to the Great Depression. Since then, its buildings have been used by a variety of businesses, including a printing company and a chemical firm that was later discovered to have contributed greatly to the pollution of the local water supply.

EDWARD HAMLIN EVERETT

1851–1929

When Henry W. Putnam Sr., one of Bennington's most generous and well-known businessmen and philanthropists and a widower, married Mary Hamlin Everett, the widow of a Cleveland physician, he took on an eleven-year-old stepson as well. Born in Cleveland on May 18, 1851, Edward Hamlin Everett was just a boy at the time of his mother's remarriage. The Hamlins were a proud family, and Edward's relations with the Putnams, including his future stepbrother Henry Putnam Jr., though warm, were often strained. Among their relatives, the Hamlins counted Mary's first cousin Hannibal Hamlin, a former governor and senator from Maine who had been vice president during Abraham Lincoln's first term. Young Everett, too, was to have his day and a large role in the town of Bennington.

When his mother and stepfather, Putnam, decided to relocate to Bennington, Edward Everett elected to remain behind in Cleveland with an uncle who was a wealthy financier. Edward visited his mother in the summers, but during the school year, he attended Andover Academy in Massachusetts. Later, he did graduate from Bennington High School with the class of 1869 while working part time for one of the Putnam enterprises in town. Returning to Cleveland, he obtained a job in a bank, but finding it uninteresting, he turned to work as a traveling representative for several glass industries, including one owned by his stepfather.

By the time he turned thirty in 1881, Everett had become the owner of his own glass factory in Newark, Ohio, some one hundred miles from

Everett Mansion. *Bennington Museum, Bennington, VT.*

Cleveland. Through hard work, he built it into a substantial business, eventually becoming known as the "Bottle King." Five years later, he actually married a King—Amy Webster King—the daughter of one of the plant's former owners. Between 1886 and 1896, the Everetts remained in Newark, and at a time when vast quantities of foods and beverages were beginning to be grown, packaged and shipped, Everett's American Bottle Company came to dominate the industry. His attention to quality and prices, as well as his ability to court such important customers as the Busch brewers, gave him a distinct edge over his competition. His concern for his employees added an important dimension to his success in business. He later pioneered businesses in natural gas and oil, and through the necessity of acquiring the sand needed for the manufacture of his glass bottles, he became interested in real estate. As a personal sideline, Everett pursued the scientific management of the fruits that filled many of his jars. Everett's four-hundred-acre farm near Newark held some twenty-five thousand fruit trees, among them apple, cherry, pear, quince, plum and peach trees.

As their fortune grew, the Everetts enjoyed an elegant life of high style and upper-class ease. Everett's three daughters, Amy, Mary and Ann, attended private schools, and their European travel was frequent. By the age of sixty, Everett had acquired a fortune estimated at some $50 million and owned properties in New York, Washington, D.C., and Switzerland in addition to Ohio. In 1910, he began building sumptuous mansions in Washington and Bennington simultaneously.

In Bennington, Edward Everett purchased a farm of several hundred acres on the east side of Mount Anthony, to which he continually added more acreage. Employing a noted architect, George Oakley Totten Jr., and importing Italian stone masons to do the job, he built a twenty-seven-room mansion in the style of a fourteenth-century Norman castle to overlook the town. The buildings are said to have cost $2 million. In 1915, the Bennington house was completed, and the family moved in. Today, after a stint as a Catholic novitiate and a college campus, the Everett estate is under development as a luxury resort. Everett's equally elegant home in Washington was also designed by Totten and has since become the Turkish Embassy.

As he had in Ohio, Everett expanded his farm in Bennington. He purchased another tract of seven hundred acres and created the world's largest privately owned orchard, planting more than eighty thousand trees. In the course of Everett's work, his estate provided ample employment for the community. He became one of the founders of the Bennington Museum and a benefactor of other local institutions. Unfortunately, his death in 1929 at the age of seventy-eight, following a second marriage late in life to Grace Burnap, an aspiring singer, prompted a highly publicized dispute over his will. But like his stepbrother Henry W. Putnam Jr., Everett is remembered as a member of a golden age in which Bennington was the host of wealthy summer visitors.

Everett's lavish mausoleum in the Park Lawn Cemetery is an exact three-quarter scale replica of the Greek Temple of Hephaestus, which still stands in Athens's ancient Agora marketplace at the base of the Acropolis. Hephaestus was the Greek name for the Roman god Vulcan, the god of fire. The tomb contains one of the largest stones ever taken from the Barre quarries. It is the capstone for the mausoleum and weighs forty-eight tons. Everett was buried inside with his two wives—something that, after the bitter conflict between their children over his will, would probably not have been their choice.

MARY ROBINSON SANFORD AND HELEN OLIVIA P. STOKES

1859–1947 AND 1870–1945

Like Samuel, John and Moses Robinson, Mary Robinson Sanford was yet another scion of the venerable Robinson family of Bennington. Although she was born in Troy on April 20, 1859, both her parents, Samuel B. and Sophia M. Bigelow Sanford, were born here. Their roots went back to Bennington's first settlers, the Robinsons, the Jennings and the Sanfords—and even beyond that to the *Mayflower* itself. Mary's father made his fortune in Troy in the manufacture of shirts and collars, earning that town the nickname of "Collar City." In addition to homes in Troy and New York City, the Sanfords bought the old brick house previously owned by Samuel Raymond on the corner of Monument Avenue and Bank Street in Bennington. There, the family spent their summers like so many of the wealthy Trojans during the Victorian era. In the years after the Civil War, Samuel and his sister Mary Sanford Robinson even owned the Walloomsac Inn before they sold it to their hotel manager, Walter Berry, around the turn of the twentieth century.

As a girl, Mary Sanford attended the Emma Willard Academy in Troy from 1869 to 1876 before she enrolled at Vassar College. As a young, wealthy socialite, she wasn't trained for any occupation, so it was unusual for her to become interested in the labor movement. She was especially concerned about low-paid workers, like the "collar girls" who were employed by her father's firm. When her mother died a few months after Mary graduated from college in 1882, she took on the responsibility of caring for her father and acted as his housekeeper.

Mary Sanford and Mary Safford on a porch in Bennington, circa 1891. *Bennington Museum, Bennington, VT.*

One of her lifelong passions was fine horses and riding, and many early photographs show her on horseback. For a short period, possibly from 1889 to 1894, she became very active as an amateur photographer. Her collection of photographs is now in the Bennington Museum, and they capture a bit of the daily lives of the wealthy families who summered here. During her photography period, Robinson was friendly with the well-known photographer Alice Austen, who gave her tips on how to make her photographs more interesting. One unique tradition that the Sanfords practiced was the firing of an old cannon that they had set up on their front lawn. It was fired twice each year: once on the day they arrived in town to herald the beginning of the summer social season and once on the day they left in the fall.

When Mary's father died unexpectedly on August 3, 1896, Mary, an only child, inherited his fortune and was then able to do whatever she wanted. She moved to New York City to live with her best friend, Mary D. Safford, and Safford's mother, Henrietta, but she continued to return to Bennington each summer. Before long, she began to buy property on the east side of Monument Circle, as well as an existing house at 34 Monument Avenue. Then in 1898, she hired architect William Bull to design a twenty-room

Shingle-style house for 7 Monument Circle. She decided to call it The Priory and moved in with at least three Black servants to take care of her. Sanford also built the carriage house that is now known as The Church Barn and a caretaker's house next to it.

In the early 1900s, Mary began to attend classes at the Rand School of Social Science in Manhattan. The school had just been founded in 1906 by a Christian Socialist minister to educate people who were interested in helping the working class establish trade unions. One of her teachers at the school was John Spargo, the same John Spargo who would later become the founder of the Bennington Museum. When Spargo was taken seriously ill in 1909, Sanford suggested that he move to the house she owned at 34 Monument Avenue. The doctors predicted that he didn't have long to live, but Spargo survived and stayed in Bennington for more than fifty years. It appears that Sanford met Helen Stokes during her Rand School period through their shared interest in socialism. Around this time, Mary Sanford and Mary Safford split up, and Sanford moved in with Stokes, joining in what was then known as a "Boston marriage" for the rest of their lives. Lesbian relationships were never mentioned in polite society during those days, but it is highly likely that the two women were more than friends.

To us today, the world of socialism seems so far from the wealth of the capitalist system that Sanford and Stokes enjoyed—a person could never be both, but it was not uncommon then. They were even given a name, "Parlor Socialists." As a spirited social reformer, Sanford was active as a sponsor for pure milk laws and anti-sweatshop legislation. While they shared a house in Greenwich Village during the winters, Mary and Helen always escaped the heat of the city in the summer. They would stay at either The Priory (which they renamed Gray Gables) or 9 Monument Circle depending on the weather. In 1931, they moved permanently to Bennington and, due to their advancing age, sold the larger Priory and lived in 9 Monument Circle when they weren't traveling. Mary Sanford died in Bennington on December 19, 1947, two years after Helen.

Helen Olivia Phelps Stokes's connection with Bennington was mainly through her association with her partner, Mary Sanford. Helen was a member of one of the wealthiest families in the country whose fortune came through the tinplate industry. One indication of the family's wealth was the summer home of her brother, Anson Phelps Stokes, in Lenox, Massachusetts. His house was called Shadow Brook, and at one time, it was the largest home in America, boasting one hundred rooms. After Anson's death, the home was opulent enough to become the summer residence of Andrew Carnegie.

Helen was born in New York on June 5, 1870, eleven years after Mary, and like Mary, she was progressive in her politics and interested in socialist theories. Another of Helen's brothers had been the founder of the Intercollegiate Socialist Society. Her father was one of the founders of the Metropolitan Museum of Art, and Helen thought of herself as an artist and portrait painter. She became a founding member of the American Civil Liberties Union in 1920 and often picketed for women's rights in New York City. The couple was well-matched.

As Helen grew older and became less mobile due to painful arthritis, Mary orchestrated their permanent move to Bennington. When Mary lost most of her money around the time of the Great Depression, Helen bought the houses and paid the bills. In their later years, they entertained people like Norman Thomas and Dorothy Canfield Fisher and took as many trips as they could. Both Helen and Mary contributed to the planning of Bennington College and were thrilled when the first students arrived. A house on the campus is named in their honor. By the time of their deaths in the 1940s, the era of Victorian summer homes was over, and the big houses they built had become too expensive to maintain.

ANNA MARY ROBERTSON "GRANDMA" MOSES

1860–1961

Grandma Moses was a local painter and member of a farming family in nearby Eagle Bridge, New York. She had strong ties to Bennington, which were confirmed when the Bennington Museum became the principal public institution to collect and display her work. This rural farm wife who seriously took up painting only in her seventies today has a gallery of her own at the Bennington Museum, and her art is known throughout the world.

Anna Mary Robertson Moses was born in 1860 in Easton, New York, just across the Vermont border near Greenwich. She made her way as a hired girl before she married Thomas Salmon Moses of Eagle Bridge. For nearly twenty years, from 1887 to 1905, she, her husband and their five surviving children lived in Virginia before they returned to Eagle Bridge. Anna and her husband were first cousins, and their children were referred to in the family as "double Moseses." After the death of her husband in 1927, Moses spent the next eight years on Elm Street in Bennington, nursing her daughter Anna, who had contracted tuberculosis. After Anna's death, Moses cared for her daughter's children until the remarriage of her son-in-law.

Today, the house in which Grandma Moses lived in Eagle Bridge is surrounded by a working farm still owned by the Moses family. Though the Moses Farm continues to be known for its own high-quality products, especially its melons and corn, the farmhouse that was lived in by Grandma Moses now sports a small barn that has been converted into a gallery for art.

Grandma Moses. *Bennington Museum, Bennington, VT.*

The work of Grandma Moses began to appear at a time when Americans had become fascinated with nostalgia and what was called "primitive" art. In the face of tremendous changes sweeping the country, Americans were beginning to see that the "improvements" they had worked so hard to achieve might force them to lose certain old-fashioned spiritual and moral qualities they held dear. Without any formal art training, folk artists like Moses were seen as representatives of a traditional, simpler way of seeing things that was fast disappearing. The simplicity and directness of naive art turned out to be its principal attraction.

In the 1930s, at the age of seventy, Grandma Moses, who had been painting for herself and her family for some time, began selling her work locally and at stores and fairs. Later, the Galerie St. Etienne in Manhattan took an interest in her art and promoted her meteoric climb to national and international fame. In October 1940, when she was eighty, she had her first solo show of work in New York City, and in 1953, she was featured on the cover of *Time* magazine.

Grandma Moses would, of course, have been popular in any case. Her charming canvases (or frequently, the more practical Masonite panels) portray a comfortable, nostalgic view of the Upper Hudson Valley, Bennington and the neighboring Green Mountains. Her depictions of horses, carriages, churches, farms, small towns and other rural appurtenances carry us back to a time when life was simpler, more peaceful. What her popularity does show is the hunger for authentic experience in a world overwrought with media, communication and public art. People who are fond of the art of Grandma Moses can visit it at the Bennington Museum and purchase it through reproductions, cards and books. They often like it for the same reason they appreciate Bennington—they enjoy a quieter and more relaxed way of life.

The paintings of Grandma Moses served her as well as they did her fans. The pace she developed for herself and the satisfaction she derived from her work seemed to succeed like the cure of the simple rural doctors she must have known. She lived to be 101 years old and died honored, respected and renowned. The Bennington Museum holds the world's largest collection of her work, and many of the paintings are nostalgic depictions of regional life. They continue to draw an appreciative public and remind us of days gone by.

WILLIAM C. BULL

1860–1934

One architect who helped shape the appearance of Bennington's streetscape more than any other was William Clark Bull. He is considered by many to be Bennington's greatest architect, and he certainly left his mark at the turn of the twentieth century by creating some of the most attractive buildings in town. Bull was born in Danby, Vermont, on February 7, 1860, and came to Bennington at the age of nineteen. After he graduated from Hungerford College in New York State with a degree in engineering, he established his first office in the First National Bank building at 332 Main Street. When Bull first lived in Bennington, he was involved in the local textile industry, but he soon devoted himself full time to architecture. On September 30, 1883, after a few years of work, Bull married Harriet Jane Scott of Bennington, and two years later, their daughter Vera Lillian Bull was born. In addition to his design business, he also became a trustee of the Village of Bennington.

Bull liked to use irregular plans and asymmetrical rooflines combined with more formal elements for decorative enrichment in his buildings. Things like columns, segmental arched entablatures and Neoclassical swags were not uncommon in his work. He built many houses in Bennington that incorporated these features, including his own house on the west corner of Pleasant and Valentine Streets. Some of the public buildings he designed and built include the Bennington Station, the Methodist church on Main Street, St. Peter's Episcopal Church on Pleasant Street and the large Town Farm building on Orchard Road. Among the grand old houses that he designed

William Bull. *Bennington Museum, Bennington, VT.*

are Mary Sibley Harwood's house at 205 Washington Avenue, Fred Graves's house at 126 Elm Street, Louis Graves's house at 124 Elm Street, the Campbell house at 207 West Main Street, Maggie Lowrie's house at 144 Union Street, Edward Bates's house at 212 Silver Street, Frank Crawford's residence at 236 Park Street, 133 Elm Street, 115 Grandview Street, Mary Sanford's house on Monument Circle and fabric designer Tzaims Luksus's Shingle-style house at the intersection of Walloomsac Road and Fairview Street.

Other houses he designed have been torn down over the past century. Graceful houses, like the Drysdale home that stood on the site of the Hotel Vervana or the Graves house on the corner of Elm and Washington Streets, where the Elks Club stands today, were replaced by more modern but less attractive buildings. Bull even designed a triumphal arch that temporarily spanned the intersection at the Four Corners during the dedication ceremonies for the Bennington Battle Monument on August 19, 1891. Although it was made completely of wood and canvas, the arch was built to resemble a stone structure that was seventy-five feet long and sixty feet high, and it was strong enough to support one hundred people.

The Bull family left town in November 1912 and moved to Brooklyn, New York. William retired from his engineering business but engaged in various other pursuits. During World War I, he was appointed chief of transportation services with the U.S. Army Ordnance Department. His work centered on the defense of Belgium, and he was made an officer of King Leopold II of Belgium. After the war, he was decorated for his service by King Albert of Belgium. For some time before his death at the age of seventy-four, he worked in Pittsburgh, experimenting with a process for the lamination of glass.

His wife of more than fifty years died on August 8, 1934, and Bull became distraught over her loss. His body was found on December 10, 1934, on the George Washington Farm near Fredericksburg, Virginia, the victim of a self-inflicted gunshot wound to the head. His friends were shocked by the news. Following his death, his body was returned to Bennington for interment in the Old Bennington Cemetery, and he was laid to rest beside his wife, Harriet.

JAMES C. COLGATE

1863–1944

The first member of the wealthy Colgate family to live in Bennington was James C. Colgate. James graduated from Madison University in 1884, before it was renamed Colgate University in his father's honor. Although he was a descendant of the soap-making Colgates, he decided to attend Columbia Law School and become a lawyer. He practiced law for only five years until 1891, when he joined his father's stock brokerage firm. His father had gone into business for himself and made a fortune during the Civil War by overseeing large exchanges of gold and paper currency.

On June 4, 1890, James married Hope Hubbell Conkling, a Bennington native, and they decided to spend their summers in Bennington, a practice they followed for the next half century. By then, James was quite wealthy, and in fact, for several years, he held the largest life insurance policy in America, with a payout of $1.5 million. He was rich enough and adventurous enough to finance Admiral Robert Peary's exploration of the Arctic, and in recognition of that, Peary named one of his discoveries Colgate Bay. Hope's family stretched back to the early days of Bennington, to Elnathan Hubbell, who had petitioned the king of England on behalf of the Bennington settlers in their disputes with the New York landlords.

The couple was married in Bennington at the Conkling family's home, which was called Benvenue. The house, a mansion that is now gone, was located on the side of Mount Anthony, on the opposite side of Route 7 from the Hubbell Homestead west of town. The wedding was reported in great detail in the *Bennington Banner* and was said to be one of "the most

James C. Colgate's Bennington home, Benvenue. *Bennington Museum, Bennington, VT.*

brilliant weddings that Bennington has ever had." Once James inherited the property from Hope's parents, he set about buying adjoining land until the farm contained nearly seven hundred acres. He spared no expense on his estate and even imported Italian stone workers to build the "Blue Stone Road" that wound for five and a half miles up the side of Mount Anthony. Then Colgate personally paid for the road between his house and downtown to be paved.

Not only did Colgate improve his own property, but he also set about improving the quality of life for the community. He and John Wool Griswold decided that the town needed a good golf course, so they bought the land and buildings where the Bennington Seminary had once stood. They turned the old school building into a clubhouse and added tennis courts. The golf course was built on Colgate's property where Camelot Village stands today. For some reason, the club was not popular enough to support itself, so Colgate and some others bought the acreage known as Clark's Woods in 1905 and raised enough money to build a new country club, one that still exists.

James also became involved in the planning of Bennington College as it was first proposed by Reverend Vincent Ravi Booth of the Old First Church. The original idea was to build the college on the grounds of their old country club on Seminary Lane so that it would be close to town. Colgate pledged to donate the land for this purpose. During the Great Depression, however, their plans changed, and Colgate rescinded his offer. In the end, the college was built on the Jennings farm in North Bennington.

James Colgate died in 1944, and in his will, he gave the right of first refusal to buy Fillmore Farms to his employees. The workers purchased it, and it became an employee-owned business under the name Fairdale Farms. It was run as a co-op for many years. Eventually, they stopped agricultural operations and converted the buildings into shops and a restaurant.

The original Benvenue House was built in 1864 for D.H. Conkling at a cost of $200,000 (millions today). Tragically, on March 9, 1899, a malfunction caused the furnace to overheat, and the building caught fire and burned to the ground. The family decided to replace it with a fifty-five-room mansion, the largest house in Bennington until the Everett House was built. As the years passed, it became too expensive to maintain, and in 1958, the house was dismantled, leaving only the gatehouse, the caretaker's house and some of the farm buildings. Building blocks from the mansion were used by the Bennington Museum in 1961 for a new addition to the galleries. The Colgates loved Bennington so much that after their deaths, they were buried in the Old Bennington Cemetery. James was described as a tower of strength and a generous and loving soul. As a testimony to Colgate's kindness and good nature, his farmworkers asked to be his pallbearers.

CHARLES CRESSON JONES

1866–1912

On May 24, 1912, a dramatic story appeared in pages of the *Bennington Banner*. It referred to an event that had occurred a month before, but it had left an indelible impression on not only Bennington but also the rest of the world. The account began: "The heroes of the world's greatest sea tragedy were not all sailors nor soldiers. There were peasants, millionaires, philanthropists, priests, actors, artists, poets, reformers, authors, editors, railroad masters, ship owners, bankers, merchants, lawyers and other's whose deeds of heroism and sacrifice challenge the martyrs of all ages. Among them was one of God's noblemen, a Vermont shepherd, C.C. Jones, of Fillmore Farms."

This sea tragedy was, of course, the sinking of the *Titanic* off the coast of Newfoundland on April 15, 1912. And Charles C. Jones was indeed a local man who had become an international hero. He was not, however—except for rhetorical purposes—simply another Vermont shepherd.

Jones was a breeder and herdsman of great stature in the agricultural community and manager of James C. Colgate's four-thousand-acre Fillmore Farms on the north slope of Mount Anthony. He had been in Britain searching for outstanding new stock for Colgate's farm. He was also assigned to engage an English housekeeper named Elizabeth Mellinger, who was traveling back to Vermont with him. That his courage was tested in the dire circumstances of the sinking of a great ship and found to be fully equal to the occasion was a surprise to no one.

Charles Cresson Jones. *Bennington Museum, Bennington, VT.*

Charles Cresson Jones was born in 1866 near Philadelphia. His father was a respected physician and medical author, and Charles, too, was trained for the medical profession. Ill health, however, forced him to seek a milder climate, and he turned to sheep and cattle ranching in Texas and Mexico. Later, he managed a large estate in Virginia before he relocated to Bennington.

Throughout his career, Jones successfully experimented with various breeds of livestock and developed regimens for their improvement and care. In southwestern Texas, beginning in the mid-1880s, he had built up, through careful selection and breeding, exceptionally heavy fleeces that were considered an extraordinary achievement in that sparse land. In Virginia, he worked to great success with new breeds, including the Shropshire and Dorset. The latter became a favorite of his.

In his work in Bennington for Colgate, Jones had pleased his employer by proving that the Dorset was a fast-growing and marketable breed. When he shipped the young lambs to New York for mutton, Jones netted an astonishing twelve dollars for each animal. Another advantage was that the nine- to eleven-week-old animals were too young to have consumed very much feed.

Jones was known as both an expert in his field and a man of compassion and good will. His ability as a raconteur made him a prized speaker at professional meetings. When the disaster struck, Jones was said to have assisted heroically in loading the *Titanic*'s lifeboats. As the last lifeboat left him to face certain death, he reportedly stood back and lit a cigar.

Jones's life recalls a time when Bennington was a haven for a number of wealthy men and their families who were rich enough to dabble in farming. Their estates still dot the landscape, and along with them come memories of men like C.C. Jones, Bennington's "Shepherd Hero of the *Titanic*." The irony of this story is that the sheep he purchased were on board another ship, and they arrived in Bennington safely. Cresson's body was found and returned for burial in the Old Bennington Cemetery.

ANNA HAWKS PUTNAM

1866–1939

In a letter to the *Bennington Banner* on January 17, 1917, Anna Hawks Putnam posed this question: "Vermont was the first state in the union to adopt universal manhood suffrage. Why not [be] the first New England state to bestow presidential suffrage upon its women? Is there a specific reason for Vermont granting this privilege to her women during this coming legislature?" To this question, she gave her own enthusiastic response: "Yes!"

Even though the suffragists' slogan for the referendum was "Vermont First," the state actually did not ratify the Nineteenth Amendment in 1920, when it was passed nationally without Vermont's help. The governor of the state, Percival Clement, was an opponent to giving women the right to vote, and as an excuse, he said that the state could not afford the cost of a special ballot. Anna Putnam continued her criticism of the governor and worked against his candidacy in the next election. One unforeseen benefit of giving women the right vote was that men were no longer allowed to spit tobacco juice on the floor at the polls.

Anna Hawks Putnam was born in Brooklyn in 1866. She moved to Bennington in 1893 with her husband, Dr. Warren E. Putnam, who practiced medicine in Hoosick, New York. By 1923, they were living in an attractive Victorian house that once stood at 122 South Street.

Although she is more widely known for her work in favor of child labor reforms, Anna was a strong advocate for women's suffrage. She was also the editor of the "Woman's Department" for *The Vermont Advance*, and in 1915 and 1916, she wrote a monthly column for the paper. Putnam explained that "all of the big questions of social import are included in the feminist agenda: temperance, peace, child labor…and so ad infinitum."

She was deeply involved in the betterment of children and women in the labor force. In 1908, she was elected the chairwoman of the Industrial and Consumer's League, a position she held for many years. Then in 1910, she was chosen as the secretary of the Vermont Branch of the National Child Labor Committee. In addition to working on child labor issues, Putnam was actively involved in both the Vermont Federation of Women's Clubs and the local Fortnightly Club, a national organization aimed at the betterment of women through education. During World War I, she served as the state chair of the Vermont Division of the Woman's Committee for the Council of National Defense.

Putnam was an accomplished speaker and lectured across the state on child labor and women's rights. Her reports centered on the harsh working conditions of children and women. In a 1909 talk on "Women in Industry," she lamented the fact that Vermont was the only New England state without laws to protect working women and proposed areas that club women might focus on. One thing that she recommended was a state department of factory and labor inspection. In an article titled "Vermont and Child Labor," published in the 1910 *Vermonter*, Putnam wrote of the deplorable labor conditions children faced daily. She said

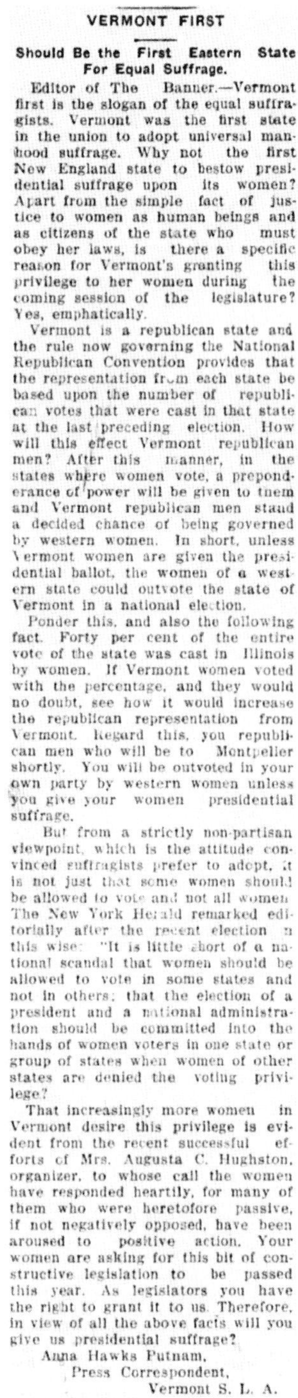

VERMONT FIRST

Should Be the First Eastern State For Equal Suffrage.

Editor of The Banner.—Vermont first is the slogan of the equal suffragists. Vermont was the first state in the union to adopt universal manhood suffrage. Why not the first New England state to bestow presidential suffrage upon its women? Apart from the simple fact of justice to women as human beings and as citizens of the state who must obey her laws, is there a specific reason for Vermont's granting this privilege to her women during the coming session of the legislature? Yes, emphatically.

Vermont is a republican state and the rule now governing the National Republican Convention provides that the representation from each state be based upon the number of republican votes that were cast in that state at the last preceding election. How will this effect Vermont republican men? After this manner, in the states where women vote, a preponderance of power will be given to them and Vermont republican men stand a decided chance of being governed by western women. In short, unless Vermont women are given the presidential ballot, the women of a western state could outvote the state of Vermont in a national election.

Ponder this, and also the following fact. Forty per cent of the entire vote of the state was cast in Illinois by women. If Vermont women voted with the percentage, and they would no doubt, see how it would increase the republican representation from Vermont. Regard this, you republican men who will be to Montpelier shortly. You will be outvoted in your own party by western women unless you give your women presidential suffrage.

But from a strictly non-partisan viewpoint, which is the attitude convinced suffragists prefer to adopt, it is not just that some women should be allowed to vote and not all women. The New York Herald remarked editorially after the recent election in this wise: "It is little short of a national scandal that women should be allowed to vote in some states and not in others; that the election of a president and a national administration should be committed into the hands of women voters in one state or group of states when women of other states are denied the voting privilege?

That increasingly more women in Vermont desire this privilege is evident from the recent successful efforts of Mrs. Augusta C. Hughston, organizer, to whose call the women have responded heartily, for many of them who were heretofore passive, if not negatively opposed, have been aroused to positive action. Your women are asking for this bit of constructive legislation to be passed this year. As legislators you have the right to grant it to us. Therefore, in view of all the above facts will you give us presidential suffrage?

Anna Hawks Putnam,
Press Correspondent,
Vermont S. L. A.

Anna Hawks Putnam's equal suffrage letter. *Bennington Museum, Bennington, VT.*

that no child should be forced to work ten or eleven hours a day, breathing harmful substances like marble dust, woolen dyes and cotton lint. She argued that those under fourteen should not be allowed to work at dangerous jobs, since the age limit at the time was twelve.

In retirement, the Putnams moved to Jackson Heights, New York City, where Anna died in 1939. She was buried in Bennington's Park Lawn Cemetery.

FRANK EDMUND HOWE

1870–1956

Of all the *Bennington Banner*'s publishers over its two centuries, Frank E. Howe was perhaps the best known, most durable and, judging by the comments in a commemorative edition published in 1953, among its most loved. Frank, known to all as "Ginger," was born in 1870 in Heath, Massachusetts, to native Vermonters who returned to the state soon after his birth. Ginger went to school in Brattleboro and learned the trade of printing early in his career. Before coming to Bennington, Howe had worked as a printer and reporter on various weeklies around the country and served as the editor of daily evening papers in Barre and Montpelier. He had covered the legislature, possessed a wide-ranging knowledge of the history and resources of Vermont and had made acquaintances throughout the state.

In December 1903, Howe combined two local publications and changed the *Banner* from a weekly to a daily publication, a measure that gave it center stage in the community and necessitated more attention to its operation, from newsgathering to the business aspects of its publication. The result was a newspaper that reflected Howe's personality and standards, and it became a mainstay in the life of the town.

Under the leadership of Ginger Howe, the *Banner* echoed a very specific character. As Luther Johnson, owner and editor of the weekly *Randolph Herald and News*, later wrote, the personality of Frank Howe figured largely in the *Banner*: "No one else thinks or writes just like Ginger. He covers his subject from his own sincere standpoint. He gives the other side a fair presentation—at least admits that the other side has something to its

Frank E. "Ginger" Howe. *Bennington Museum, Bennington, VT.*

credit. This editor never needs to initial his matter—readers recognize it as easily as his face." Governor Lee Emerson wrote that Howe's broad knowledge of Vermont affairs gave considerable prestige to his editorial opinions and that his personal columns were known throughout the state.

Howe did not manage the paper alone. He was joined by a veritable dynasty of Howes. First came his eldest son, Edmund, who managed the *Banner* from 1924 to 1930, and then his younger son Paul assumed the duties of publisher after his brother's early death at the age of thirty-five. Paul continued the family's management, but he did not outlive his father either. After Paul's death, the paper was managed by Ginger's grandson, Edmund's son Frank E. Howe II. Ginger Howe died in Bennington on July 20, 1956, and was buried in Park Lawn Cemetery.

Outside his work at the *Banner*, Ginger had a career in politics. He returned to Montpelier in 1908, this time not as a reporter but as a legislator. As a freshman in the legislature, he offered a bill to give Vermonters the right to elect their governor directly rather than through delegates. He also proposed a bill for a new county courthouse and jail, which was needed in Bennington. Howe was known as a conservative Republican who also knew how to represent upstate commercial interests. While serving in Montpelier, he was elected speaker of the House of Representatives from 1910 to 1912, and from 1912 to 1915, he was lieutenant governor and thus presided over the Vermont Senate. In the 1918 Republican primary, Howe was defeated by the publisher of the *Rutland Herald*, Percival W. Clement, who later went on to become governor. From 1923 to 1933, Howe held the position of postmaster for Bennington, appointed by President Coolidge.

The Howe years at the *Banner* were eventful ones, with two world wars, the Great Depression, the New Deal and the beginning of the postwar era dominating the news. Scions of the Putnam and Colgate families were still active in the affairs of the town. The local insurance agent, William H. Wills, became the governor, and in 1923, the nation had a Vermont president by the name of Calvin Coolidge. Howe's son Edmund had a personal connection with the new president, too. Edmund had been one of the few eyewitnesses to Coolidge's early-morning inauguration in Plymouth, Vermont, following the death of Warren Harding. His report of the event was published in the *Ludlow Tribune*, of which he was then editor.

In 1960, the *Banner* was sold to Lawrence K. "Pete" Miller and Donald B. Miller, publishers of the *Berkshire Eagle* in Pittsfield, Massachusetts, one of the best small newspapers of its day. The Millers brought the *Banner* into the present day. Pete Miller pioneered offset printing in New England and oversaw the development of the *Banner* to a high level of professionalism before it was sold again in the 1990s.

ROBERT FROST

1874–1963

We all know Robert Frost—or believe we do. Most think of Frost as the four-time winner of the Pulitzer Prize; as the contentious opponent of blank verse, over whose merits he argued with T.S. Eliot; as the crusty New Englander who wrote about stone walls and neighbors; and as the poet who offered a new and significant poem at the 1961 inauguration of President John F. Kennedy.

To the surprise of many, an accurate picture of the poet's life would be quite different. Frost was born and spent his early years not in New England but in California. His father, William Frost Jr., was not a typical New England conservative but rebelled in a way that perhaps presages some of the attitudes of his son. In the middle of the nineteenth century, he moved to San Francisco to work as a journalist on a Democratic newspaper. During the Civil War, he had been sympathetic to the Southern cause. His son, the poet, was born on March 26, 1874, and was given the full name Robert Lee Frost, after the famous general who had led the armies of the Confederacy. Thus, the figure connected so closely with New England independence might well be considered, instead, an early product of the flamboyant and complex new state of California.

Further confounding expectation, Frost was not originally acclaimed in this country; instead, he was first renowned in England, where he lived for three years in his mid-thirties. It was not until he returned home in 1915, after the publication of *A Boy's Will* (1913) and *North of Boston* (1914), that he was accorded the status his twenty years of writing poetry deserved. From

Robert Frost. *Bennington Museum, Bennington, VT.*

that time on, he was known principally as a poet, though he also spent a significant portion of his time teaching and lecturing.

Prior to his time in England, Frost had farmed briefly in New Hampshire and taught school to support himself and his family. He had also worked at such quintessential nineteenth- and early twentieth-century occupations as bobbin boy and shoemaker, as well as editor of a newspaper.

In 1920, Frost had to commit his younger sister to a mental hospital, where she died a few years later. That same year, he moved with his wife and family into the beautiful Stone Cottage, which can still be seen on Route 7A in South Shaftsbury. There, in June 1922, he wrote one of his best-known works, "Stopping by Woods on a Snowy Evening," a poem Frost described as having been written in one sitting between first light and the rising of the sun. Finding the old stone cottage too close to the increasing traffic on the road and overly available to the public, Frost gave it to his son, Carol Frost, and moved to a quieter farm he dubbed The Gulley a mile to the north. The Gulley became the Frost home for a decade, from 1928 to 1938. While living there, he wrote a number of works, including the humorous "A Record Stride" and the lengthy "Build Soil—A Political Pastoral." The poet attracted a steady stream of colleagues and admirers to The Gulley, until the farm was sold in 1963 to painter Kenneth Noland and again in 1979 to television producer Norman Lear.

Frost considered himself a Vermonter despite the considerable time he spent away lecturing and teaching at colleges around the country. He remained a Shaftsbury voter until 1948, and the grave he shares with his wife and children, one of the most visited in the nation, lies in the cemetery next to the Old First Church in Bennington. The granite slab, bordered with simple carved leaves, records the date of his death, January 29, 1963, and bears the celebrated, almost Shakespearean line, "I had a lover's quarrel with the world."

In the past, there was hardly a schoolchild who could not recite Frost's "Stopping by Woods on a Snowy Evening" or expound on Frost's rustic views of neighbors and friends. Frost was, however, a complex figure and hid the subtleties of his character behind his façade of a simple New Englander. Ruth Levin captures this in her brief sketch of Frost for a history of Shaftsbury called *Ordinary Heroes*. When asked by some well-intentioned questioner whether he was an introvert or an extrovert, Frost considered this obviously overly intellectualized question and replied that he was just a "plain vert, from Vermont."

JOHN SPARGO

1876–1966

One of the more interesting and diverse biographies that make up the history of Bennington is that of John Spargo, the founder and director of the Bennington Museum. Born to Thomas and Jane Spargo, a stonemason and his wife in Cornwall, England, on January 31, 1876, John Spargo learned the craft of stonecutting from his father. He was largely self-educated and left school at the age of fourteen. He later became involved with the labor movement, Marxism in particular. At the same time, he also preached as a Methodist lay minister. In 1894–95, he took two courses with the Oxford University's Extension Program and embraced Christian Socialism as a means of helping the working man.

Spargo soon left the church to devote himself to labor full time. For the next twenty years, Spargo was heavily involved in the socialist movement and the causes of labor and reform. From 1896 to 1901, he served on the executive council of the Social Democratic Federation. He helped found the Federation of Trades and Labor Councils and held several related posts. By the turn of the twentieth century, he was an acknowledged socialist intellectual with special skills of memory and oratory.

In 1900, Spargo married Prudence Edwards, and in early 1901, the couple sailed to the United States to give a series of lectures on the labor movement. The lecture series didn't pan out, but the Spargos settled in New York City, where he edited a radical journal called *The Comrade* and published it as widely as he could. Prudence died of tuberculosis in 1904, and shortly thereafter, John married Mary Amelia Rose Bennetts. John's book *The Bitter*

John Spargo. *Bennington Museum, Bennington, VT.*

Cry of the Children, published in 1906, condemned child labor and became a best-seller. The book was meant to influence attitudes and change legislation in this country.

In 1907, Spargo became an American citizen, and he and his wife, Mary, moved to Bennington in the winter of 1909, hoping that the climate would help his heart and lung problems, even though doctors had given him only a few weeks to live due to a severe bout with pneumonia. Mary Sanford and Helen Stokes, wealthy friends from New York, had been students of his at the Rand School of Social Science, and they owned a summer home in Bennington. They invited Spargo to convalesce rent-free in a small house that Mary owned at 34 Monument Avenue. Not only did John survive his illness, but he lived in that same house, which he called Nestledown, for the next fifty-seven years until his death at the age of ninety.

Once in Bennington, Spargo continued his support of socialist causes, but his views from then on shifted increasingly to the right. Though he continued to write more books on Marx and socialism, the advent of World War I and the aftermath of the Russian Revolution eventually turned Spargo toward a more conciliatory stance. In 1916, he joined a small group that included the writer Upton Sinclair in resigning from the Socialist Party. In the following years, he turned again to the cause of labor, revising and softening his political views. Soon, he was consulting on policy with the government of Woodrow Wilson. By the mid-1920s, he began following a path he called "socialized individualism" and eventually became a Republican. By the 1930s, he had turned against socialism and was speaking out against progressive programs like the New Deal.

As he retreated from left-wing politics, Spargo began to embrace local history and tradition. From his vantage point in Bennington, he took a new interest in early American history, writing dozens of books of local interest. He wrote about Bennington's battle flag and became an expert in the history of the town's potteries and other subjects of regional interest. In 1926, he helped found the Bennington Museum through the generosity of James C. Colgate and Edward H. Everett, and when its doors opened on August 16, 1928, Spargo was its first director. He became president of the Vermont Historical Society, a position he retained until 1938. From 1925 to 1927, he headed the Vermont Sesquicentennial Commission, and in 1931, he was active on the George Washington Bicentennial Committee.

These were astonishing changes for someone who began his life as an uneducated mine worker and an outspoken radical. By 1954, when he retired from the museum, Spargo was known more for his historical work than his politics. Today, Spargo's books serve as important though highly opinionated sources for local history and its interpretation. And the museum he helped found is visited by thousands each year. Following a decade of retirement, Spargo died on August 17, 1966, a day after the 189th celebration of the Battle of Bennington. His final interests included gardening, a subject blessedly beyond politics, and the history of the town he had come to love.

VINCENT RAVI BOOTH

1876–1950

Vincent Ravi Booth was the pastor remembered as the prime mover behind the founding of Bennington College and the restoration of Old Bennington's historic post-Revolutionary Old First Church to its original appearance. These were two key aspects in the development of Bennington in the 1930s. Together, they helped make Bennington what it is today.

Born in Naples, Italy, on July 20, 1876, as Vincent Booth Ravi, he was the son of an Italian father and a Scottish mother. As an adult, in a characteristically idiosyncratic gesture, he reversed his parents' names at the time of World War I, giving prominence to the name of his mother. It was his protest against the Italian politics of the day. Booth's father was also an independent thinker who had originally been ordained as a Catholic priest, but he later embraced Protestantism and became the pastor of a Methodist church in Florence. Having attended a Methodist conference in the United States in 1893, the elder Booth decided to send Vincent and his sister to college at Ohio Wesleyan University. After working his way through school, Vincent chose to stay in America. He earned a theological degree from Boston University, and in 1901, was ordained a minister in the Methodist Episcopal Church. In 1905, he became an American citizen. Prior to coming to Bennington in 1919, Booth had been the pastor of Manchester's Congregational churches from 1906 to 1909, and then he became the pastor in Cambridge, Massachusetts, until 1919, when he came to Bennington.

While unconventional thinking may have been characteristic of Booth and his family, Booth also possessed tenacity. Each year after he arrived in Bennington, Booth noticed that as the summer season faded, so did his congregation. Because of railroads and the automobile, Old Bennington had increasingly become a vacation colony. As winter approached, the old houses were closed, and his parishioners returned to their permanent homes in the cities of the Northeast and Midwest. In the early 1920s, Booth and his wife, Miriam, came up with of a plan to solve the problem of their dwindling congregation numbers. If they started a school for girls, the students would fill the seasonal void, and additionally, the faculty and staff would make good year-round members. For the next ten years, Booth worked ceaselessly to bring this idea to life.

Initially, Booth envisioned a traditional school in Old Bennington. He thought he would either create a school or convince an established school to relocate to Bennington, which he portrayed as idyllic and highly suitable to the aims of education. He set about locating buildings and land and raising funds. He secured the interest of potential donors and trustees and expanded his speculations with forays into educational theory.

Once he began speaking directly with educators, Booth found the intensity of his interest returned. Over the years, he found that his plans had changed somewhat. By 1925, when the college was chartered, and certainly by 1932 when the first students arrived, Booth's traditional college idea had morphed into a school that aggressively championed the education of women, organized along lines that were radical for the day. In the end, the offer from James C. Colgate of 45 acres of land in Old Bennington for the campus was withdrawn, but in its place, Laura Hall Park Jennings, the daughter of Trenor Park, agreed to donate 140 acres a few miles away in North Bennington. That location was agreed upon, and although Booth became less involved with the college, his efforts to establish it are acknowledged by all. His legacy includes the addition of some prominent faculty members and staff to the community. The school might not have helped build his congregation, but it certainly has helped the town.

Booth's second great accomplishment was the restoration of the Old First Church to its original 1805 appearance. Over the years, it had been greatly changed and "modernized" in a Victorian fashion, often with little appreciation of the simpler beauty of the church's interior space. Noting that the Old First Church would better represent the town's Revolutionary past if returned to its original state, Booth set about raising funds for its restoration. Motivated by a love for his community and the church's history, as well as the popularity of architectural revival at that time, Booth was able to raise the necessary money, and the renovations were completed in 1937. The building was rededicated as "Vermont's Colonial Shrine," ignoring the fact that Vermont had never been one of the original colonies, so technically, it could not be "colonial."

Booth's relationships with members of the Old Bennington community and the wealthy summer crowd from New York made it possible for him to succeed in his projects. Few would deny him the key elements of spirit, imagination and style that helped him make Bennington more attractive and functional for visitors and residents alike. He died the day after Christmas 1950 and was buried with his wife in Manchester's Dellwood Cemetery.

DOROTHY CANFIELD FISHER

1879–1958

Dorothea "Dorothy" Frances Canfield was named for the heroine of George Eliot's novel *Middlemarch*, Dorothea Brooke, foretelling the literary path she would take herself on. Her father was a college professor in Kansas, and even though she was born in that state, she had deep family roots in Vermont and was well known in Bennington County. As a little girl, she and her mother frequently visited her Canfield relatives in Arlington while on summer vacations.

In 1907, after graduating from Columbia College with a doctorate in French, she married John Fisher, and together, they had two children. In 1911, a few years after her graduation, she visited Rome, and there, she learned about educator Maria Montessori and her groundbreaking work with children at the Casa dei Bambini. Montessori believed in letting children do independent work so they could engage with the world directly instead of focusing on regimented classroom studies. Fisher admired Montessori's methods and absorbed her teachings to such a degree that once she was back in America, she translated several of Montessori's books into English. Throughout her life, in addition to being a great proponent of the "Montessori Method," Dorothy was deeply involved with the education of both children and adults. Throughout World War I she worked with refugee children in Europe and helped establish a Braille press for the benefit of those who lost their sight during the war.

Following their return from the war, the Fishers moved from New York City to Vermont, where they remained for the rest of their lives. The house they lived in was located on property that had been owned by the Canfield family

Dorothy Canfield Fisher and John Fisher by Norman Rockwell, circa 1950. *Artwork courtesy of the Norman Rockwell Family Agency.*

since 1764. Dorothea also inherited her aunt Martha's home on Arlington's Main Street, which had been her grandparents' house. She donated it to the town for use as a library and community center and even supplied it with books. When her only son was killed in the Philippines during World War II, she donated funds in his memory to help build a school and playground for the village children.

Fisher became absorbed in all kinds of social work and directed her efforts especially toward education. She was appointed to the Vermont Board of Education in 1919, and with that agency, she worked for the improvement of rural education throughout the state. She was able to finance her volunteer work with money earned through her writing and editorial work. In 1921 her book *The Brimming Cup* was published and sold more copies than any other book that year except *Main Street* by Sinclair Lewis. The novel exposes the discriminatory treatment of Black people in Georgia and was singled out by professor Janis Stout as "the first modern best-seller to present criticism of racial prejudice."

To the outside world, Dorothy was known as a prolific and best-selling author, writing more than forty books. Many of those books attempted to popularize life in Vermont and helped lead to an increase in tourism in the state. Other titles warned against all forms of prejudice and racial injustice and urged for prison reform. She was even a longtime trustee of Howard University, one of the nation's historically Black colleges.

At one point, she served as president of the Adult Education Association. She wrote books for children, books on education, collections of short stories and books extolling Vermont values and traditions. Since Dorothea needed more room in which to work, John built an addition to their small house solely for her to write in. They were both internationalists and traveled throughout the world, but Dorothea always returned to Arlington to write.

Dorothea was also a founding member of the Book of the Month Club from its beginnings in 1926 until 1951, and she was the only woman on its board for those twenty-five years. She was known to read an average of fifteen books a month, and mail and manuscripts arrived constantly at her house. Through her recommendation of books for the club, she helped shape the popular reading tastes of the nation. In 1945, she championed Richard Wright's book *Black Boy* and wrote an introduction for it. Her work to bring equal opportunities to minorities and women was noted by Eleanor Roosevelt, who named her one of the ten most influential women in America.

Vermont owes a debt to Dorothy Fisher for bringing many of her friends to the state, either as visitors or residents. She touted the Bennington area to Robert Frost and recommended the house he purchased in South Shaftsbury. Her friendship with Norman and Mary Rockwell helped them decide to move to Arlington as well. Books such as her *Memories of Arlington, Vermont*, published in 1957, brought additional visitors to the state, and tourism gave the state an economic shot in the arm. She suggested that tourist revenues should be used to help finance the state's educational and social needs.

To quote her obituary in the *Bennington Evening Banner*: "Education and young people were two of her greatest interests. She believed that the hope for a peaceful world rested upon a well-informed younger generation." It is ironic that recent claims have been made criticizing Fisher for depicting minorities with stereotypes that are insulting by today's standards. The negative criticism has been reinforced by the discovery that Fisher was one of the seventy people who contributed writing to the 1931 publication *Rural Vermont: A Program for the Future.* That book was edited by Henry F. Perkins, a University of Vermont professor who proposed eugenics as a solution to the problem of mental illness, an unpopular approach today. She was also on a board called The Vermont Commission on Country Life, which Perkins headed. A movement to change the name of the Dorothy Canfield Fisher Book Award was successful as a result of these affiliations.

Dorothy Canfield Fisher died in Arlington on November 9, 1958, at the age of seventy-nine. Her husband, John, followed her in death the next year. She was buried next to the tiny church on the Arlington village green.

MARY AMELIA ROSE BENNETTS SPARGO AND MARY SPARGO

1880–1953 AND 1904–1991

Bennington Museum director John Spargo's second wife, Mary, deserves recognition in her own right. Although her death certificate lists her occupation as "housewife," she accomplished much more in her life. Mary Amelia Rose Bennetts was born in London on May 11, 1880, but she came to America when she was two years old. In 1904, while working in a carpet factory, she met and, the following year, married John Spargo, who, by then, was a well-known socialist and labor activist. A year later, the couple moved into a settlement house in Yonkers, and Mary Amelia gave birth to their only surviving daughter, also named Mary. A son named John had died in childhood, and another son died during World War II.

Mary Amelia Bennetts's political views were much more conservative than John's. She is given credit for moving him away from his extreme revolutionary theories to a more moderate reformist socialism. When the couple moved to Bennington in 1909 to take advantage of Mary Sanford and Helen Stokes's generous offer of a house on Monument Avenue, Mary Amelia Spargo began to play a larger role in the women's suffrage movement. She became the auditor for the Vermont Equal Suffrage Association in 1917 and served as vice president of the Bennington Woman Voter's Association. She was instrumental in organizing the March of Four Hundred Women to Montpelier on April 21, 1920, to lobby for a woman's right to vote. Even though she collected thousands of signatures on a petition in favor of gaining the vote, Vermont failed to ratify the Nineteenth Amendment to the Constitution. Equal suffrage for women took up most of her energies

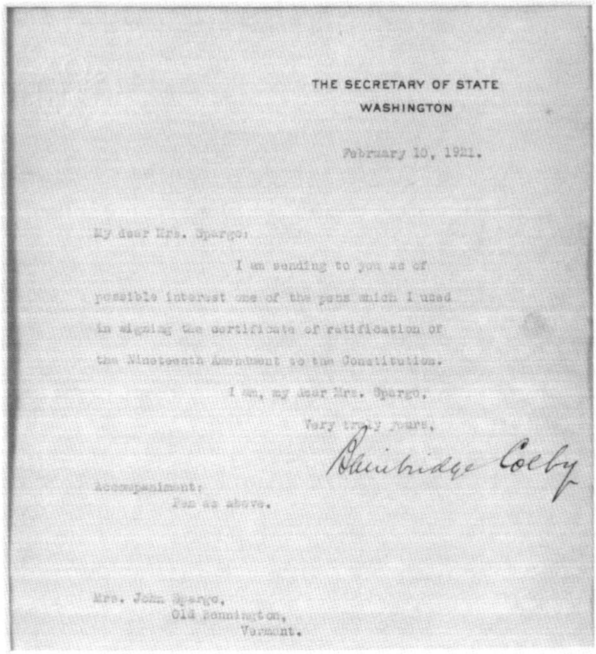

THE SECRETARY OF STATE
WASHINGTON

February 10, 1921.

My dear Mrs. Spargo:

I am sending to you as of possible interest one of the pens which I used in signing the certificate of ratification of the Nineteenth Amendment to the Constitution.

I am, my dear Mrs. Spargo,

Very truly yours,

Bainbridge Colby

Accompaniment:
Pen as above.

Mrs. John Spargo,
Old Bennington,
Vermont.

Pen and letter given to Mary Spargo by Bainbridge Colby in recognition of her work toward women's suffrage in Vermont. *Bennington Museum, Bennington, VT.*

in those years, and she attended every Vermont Equal Suffrage Association conference held between 1916 and 1920, serving as the organization's auditor in 1919 and 1920. So important was Mary Amelia in the struggle to secure the right to vote that she was one of only three people to receive a ceremonial pen that was used to sign the suffrage legislation.

Mary Amelia later became involved in other activities that included membership in the local Community Choral Club and the Fortnightly Club.

Her relationship with her husband appeared to many to be rocky at best. He seemed to be self-absorbed and oblivious to her needs. She once was quoted as saying, "John married me because he needed a cheap nursemaid." Mary Amelia died in Bennington on February 17, 1953, of a blood clot in her heart more than a decade before her husband.

Mary Amelia and John Spargo's daughter was also named Mary, and she grew up with them in their home at 34 Monument Avenue in Bennington. She was born on July 5, 1904, and educated here. After she graduated from the University of Vermont, she worked for several newspapers around New England before joining the *Washington Post* in 1942. She worked as the Capitol Hill correspondent, and she was assigned to cover the House Un-American Activities Committee during the anticommunist scare created by Joseph McCarthy and Richard Nixon later in the 1940s and 1950s. Her columns featured reports of the subpoenas served to the thirty film stars who were investigated by the HUAC. Ten of those people refused to answer committee questions, resulting in them being blackballed from the industry and their lives being destroyed. They are known now as the Hollywood Ten. Spargo also covered the testimony of Whitaker Chambers for the newspaper. He was the person who exposed Alger Hiss as a communist spy in another famous trial.

In 1950, Mary Spargo left the *Post* and went to work for the Washington, D.C. chapter of the American Red Cross. She then took up the job of public relations director for the Daughters of the American Revolution, while at the same time, she was secretly working as an informant for the FBI. She moved to Albany in 1958 to be closer to her aging father and worked for the *Albany Times Union* until her retirement in 1977. She died on September 24, 1991.

WILLIAM HENRY WILLS

1882–1946

William H. Wills, the most recent Benningtonian to be elected governor, served during World War II and was one of the town's foremost civic and business leaders. Born in 1882 in Chicago to parents who were temporarily displaced from Vermont, Wills made the return trip from Illinois to Vergennes, his family's home, in 1892 at the age of ten. With him were his brother and sister and his recently widowed mother. Their food supplies for the long trip were packed neatly in a shoebox. Throughout the many successes and challenges he would experience during his career, Wills would always think of this moment of adversity as one of the formative points in his life.

Once back in Vergennes, Wills's mother worked as a laundress. Wills himself delivered newspapers and later worked in a nail factory to earn additional income for his family. Eventually, he took a job as a store clerk for three dollars a week. In his free time, he paid twelve dollars to take a correspondence course in sales, administration and finance, which he said was probably the best money he ever spent.

Seizing an opportunity to improve himself, Wills moved to Bennington and found a job. He continued to support his family in Vergennes until he was able to bring them to Bennington. Before long, Wills had carved out a place for himself in the shoe department at Drysdale's, Bennington's preeminent dry goods and department store. When his brother arrived, he found work for him there as well. While working at Drysdale's, Bill saw the need for a reliable insurance agency in town. He tried to juggle his schedule,

William Henry Wills. *Bennington Museum, Bennington, VT.*

but his insurance occupation eventually came into conflict with his work at Drysdale's. He soon found himself out of a regular job, but his insurance business was growing, and before long, his financial situation was mended. It had been a peaceful separation, and even though Wills had lost his job at Drysdale's, Mr. Drysdale became one of his insurance customers.

From 1915 to 1931, Wills spent most of his energy developing the William H. Wills Insurance Agency in various offices along Main Street before building his own office in 1950 on South Street directly across from Drysdale's. He became active on the boards of other local companies and organizations and began to involve himself in politics. During this time, he developed friendships and allegiances that would stand him in good stead throughout his career.

In 1931, Wills ran for lieutenant governor for the first time. Though he was energetic and devoted to his campaign, he lost. This experience, combined with an operation for a suspected cancer that left him with a disability, forced him to rethink his priorities and to refocus his energies more carefully. Returning to his work, he led his insurance agency through the difficult years of the Great Depression and, in 1936, won election as lieutenant governor under Governor George Aiken.

In 1940, with the same enthusiasm he had devoted to his race for lieutenant governor four years earlier, Wills ran for governor of Vermont on the Republican ticket. He won handily and served from 1941 to 1945. Using his business experience and showing a concern for the underprivileged, Governor Wills consolidated government operations and made them more efficient. He worked closely with the legislature and department heads in Montpelier and mediated several important labor disputes.

Wartime offered the governor new challenges and a need for austerity. He learned to make good use of what little resources were available. In 1943, he canceled the inaugural ball for his second term and dictated that celebratory events be staged in a simpler manner. It was then that the Von Trapp family arrived in Vermont from war-torn Europe, and they appeared for the governor at a public party held in Montpelier. Wills's wife, Hazel McLeod, wrote a charming biography of her husband called *Bill Wills and Company* and followed in her husband's footsteps after his death on March 6, 1946, serving as state senator from Bennington County from 1961 to 1963.

Among Governor Wills's major accomplishments was an increase in government support for the University of Vermont. For this, he was gratefully awarded an honorary degree. He retired after his second term as governor, but health considerations prevented him from running for the U.S. Senate, as he had planned. He was appointed to the Federal Communications Commission but died in 1946 soon after his appointment while presiding over one of the commission's meetings in Brockton, Massachusetts. He was buried in the Park Lawn Cemetery in Bennington.

His honorary degree speaks as an appropriate epitaph:

> *His Excellency, William Henry Wills, governor of Vermont. Coming to the state in boyhood and sharing ever since then its life, turning in his middle years to public service in House and Senate and finally in his present office; as legislator and executive, ever mindful of the people's needs, facing gallantly the issue of our University's continued career and offering himself as her champion, thus bringing other true men to her aid by his challenge to their courage and self-respect.*

The same might be said of his service to the community as a whole.

MARY ROGERS

1883–1905

It might seem strange to consider a woman who was executed for the murder of her husband for inclusion in a book like this, but the case of Mary Rogers captivated the imaginations of the people of Bennington for years, and she was a great influence on the lives of many people in the town. Before Mary Rogers, only one woman in Vermont had ever faced the death penalty; Mary became the last woman to be executed by hanging in the state. In a 1953 anniversary edition of the *Bennington Banner*, it wrote that "perhaps the story that brought more excitement, intrigue and nationwide attention to this community was the famed Mary Rogers murder case. Readers throughout the nation followed the case for nearly three full years."

Born on March 9, 1883, in Hoosick, New York, as Mary Bennett to a father who was described as a mentally ill alcoholic, she was repeatedly abused as a child. Her mother was considered mentally deficient and died when Mary was six months old. Her father tried to kill Mary more than once, according to reports. Mary was just a girl of fifteen when she married Marcus Rogers, and early in their marriage, Mary began to regret it. At the age of eighteen, Mary had a daughter, but she was not a fit mother and admitted that she dropped the newborn baby on its head. The baby died of a fractured skull shortly afterward. Her husband's family always believed that the death was not an accident but intentional.

It appears that Marcus loved Mary, but she wanted her freedom. He found a job in Hoosick Falls, but Mary moved to Bennington and took up relationships with various men. At one point, it appears that Mary had tried

Above: Mary Rogers. *Courtesy of the* Bennington Banner.

Opposite: Mary Rogers on the gallows. *Courtesy of the* Bennington Banner.

to poison Marcus, but failing in that, she asked Levi Perham to kill him for part of the money she would receive from his life insurance policy. Levi turned down the offer, but Mary persisted and enlisted Levi's brother, Leon Perham, as her accomplice, even though she told him that she wanted Marcus out of the way so that she could marry yet a third man, Morris Knapp. It was all very much like a soap opera.

On the evening of August 11, 1902, Mary lured her husband into a secluded area in Bennington, and with Leon's help, she bound his hands and chloroformed him. Thinking that they could make it look like a drowning, they pushed his dead body into the river near the East Main Street bridge over the Walloomsac at Beech Street, just behind today's Miller's Toll cocktail bar. They prepared a note to leave nearby with his hat in a feeble attempt to make it appear like he had died by suicide. The police found his body on August 12, and at first, they believed that Marcus had taken his own life. Once they began to investigate the death, however, it was easily identified as a murder. Perham made a quick confession and became the key witness against Mary.

The trial began in the Bennington Courthouse in December 1903, and just before Christmas, the jury returned with their verdict with more than one thousand people crowded into the courtroom and gathered outside. Leon Perham was found guilty and sentenced to life imprisonment with hard labor. Mary Rogers was found guilty of murder in the first degree and was sentenced to death.

Efforts were made to commute Mary's sentence, but they all failed, even on appeal to the U.S. Supreme Court. The dramatic events continued when Mary was found to have had sexual relations while in prison, and she gave birth to another child after she had been jailed for more than a year. On December 8, 1905, having exhausted all hopes for clemency, Mary Rogers, by then twenty-two years old, was hanged in the Vermont State Prison in

No last reprieve

By BOB WILLIAMS

"Please see that my sister gets these"

Mary disposes of her eyeglasses just before her execution. (an engraving)

Windsor. Yet again, things went badly for her. The rope failed to snap her neck as it should have, and she struggled for fourteen minutes before her death. This was the last time hanging was used as a means of execution in the state.

Her case was so sensational that it made headlines everywhere. People from across the country expressed their opinions about whether a woman should be executed or not. Thirty thousand people in Cincinnati signed a petition to ask Governor Charles Bell to show mercy. He stayed her execution three times, but the story dragged on and on. The intrigue continued, and three attempts were made to poison Mary while she was in prison. It is worth noting that in Bennington, the first issue of the *Bennington Banner* as a daily newspaper came out on the first day of the Rogers trial. Until then, it had been a weekly.

HAZEL McLEOD WILLS

1886–1969

Even though Hazel McLeod, the future wife of Governor Wills, was born in Goldsboro, North Carolina, she was a near-lifelong resident of Bennington. She graduated from Middlebury College with the class of 1909 and then married Bill Wills on August 19, 1914, settling permanently in Bennington. At first, she taught Latin in the newly built Bennington High School on East Main Street, but as her husband became more involved in state politics, she took on more volunteer service roles. For many years, she served as a trustee for both Bennington College and the University of Vermont. Education was so important to her that after her death in 1969, the American Association of University Women created the Hazel Wills Memorial Prize, which is given annually to an outstanding woman educator in Vermont.

Hazel Wills. *Bennington Museum, Bennington, VT.*

Following her husband's death in 1946, Hazel followed in his political footsteps and was elected the state senator from Bennington. Many people eagerly read her opinion column in the *Bennington Banner*, often filled with reminiscences of days gone by. Hazel continued to write those columns until her own death in 1969. She divided her time between acting as chairman of the Vermont Library Commission and her tenure as president of the Vermont Association for the Crippled. She was the founder and director of the Bennington United Counseling Service. Hazel was also active in the Women's Auxiliary of the Episcopal Diocese of Vermont, the Bennington Club, the Bennington Garden Club, the Community Chest and Forums Inc. For a while, she was even treasurer of the Bennington County Republican Club.

No one will ever know how Hazel Wills found time to write and publish a book as well, but in 1953, she did just that. It was a brief biography of her husband's work that she titled *Bill Wills and Company.*

KARL HAMLEN MARTIN

1888–1954

Most Benningtonians today are unaware that a local company produced one of the most ambitious and stylish automobiles of the 1920s, a time in which the automobile was relatively new and excitement about its future possibilities was great.

Bennington's automobile, the Wasp, was the brainchild of Karl Martin. An early advocate of automotive development and design, Martin was a professional designer, engineer and builder who specialized in automobile coachwork. Born in Buffalo in 1888, he began his career in 1912 after graduating from St. Paul's School in New Hampshire. Automobiles were in his blood. It is reported that his father, Dr. Truman Martin, was the first person to purchase automobile insurance in America in 1897. His son continued to pursue automobile design while serving in the Aviation Department of the U.S. Navy through World War I. At the end of the war, Martin worked in New York and Chicago before he moved to Bennington, where he began to design and build the first of six automobiles. Bennington was the home of his maternal grandparents, and he knew that "labor in Bennington was both skilled and cheap." On June 2, 1919, Martin, Robert Healy and E.H. Holden formed the Martin-Wasp Corporation and sold stock in the company at $100 per share. The company rented part of Olin Scott's old foundry building on Pleasant Street and began to order parts for about six cars.

During this era, Bennington was devoting considerable attention to the automobile. As a major crossroads for the increasingly traveled highways

Karl Martin and his Wasp. *Bennington Museum, Bennington, VT.*

leading north and south, connecting Burlington and Montreal with New York, and east and west to Boston and Albany, the town was proud of its title as the "Gateway to Vermont." As use of the automobile continued to expand, eventually displacing the area's successful but inherently limited street rail system, Bennington's role as a stopping point, destination and shipping center grew. By 1925, the year the last Wasp was produced, a promotional brochure for Bennington listed some eight garages at the center of town that sold and serviced fifteen different brands of cars, including not only Chrysler, Buick and Chevrolet, but also Harley-Davidson and Rolls-Royce. One of these showrooms, sumptuous for its time, was the former Bennington Garage, which now serves as the local branch of the community college system of Vermont.

The first Wasp produced by Martin was exhibited in January 1920 during National Automobile Week at the Commodore Hotel in New York City. Its fine craftsmanship and striking design made it popular with the public. The actor Douglas Fairbanks loved it so much that he immediately bought it for his fiancée, Mary Pickford. Over the next five years, Martin refined the

Wasp's design while using the best quality materials available and displaying the most scrupulous possible care to construction. It had a powerful engine, similar to those that powered the more famous Stutz vehicles. Its carefully engineered frame and light wire wheels offered the firmness and safety that were needed at the speeds it was capable of—if suitable roads could be found. Its coachwork was, of course, the direct responsibility of Karl Martin.

One of the distinguishing characteristics of the Wasp was Martin's skill in offering potential buyers the personalized details they desired. In beautiful drawings that still exist, Martin would sketch out a vehicle for each client; each of his automobiles was unique. In comparison to other automobiles of the day, the Wasp was also strikingly modern in its lines and details. Its fenders had a distinctive angular style and its radiator logo resembled a piece of modern art. Each car came with a St. Christopher's medal as standard equipment. Even its toolbox, which was mounted in such a way that it penetrated the plane of the running board, was apparently installed in adherence more to an esthetic than a practical standard.

Poor business conditions and difficulty in obtaining capital slowed Martin's progress. No Wasps were assembled after 1925, and the total production of these superb vehicles amounted to only sixteen. Martin did not believe in the new art of advertising, so his marketing attempts were limited. At a time when nearly forty new brands of automobiles were introduced per year, the Wasp was promoted largely through word of mouth. Martin's business continued to produce specialty parts and castings, but it finally closed in 1932, due in part to the onset of the Great Depression. The last Wasp produced can be seen on display at the Bennington Museum, a tribute to traditional Vermont craftsmanship reflected in the new, industrial guise it took on in the early twentieth century. Martin died on July 6, 1954, after a long illness and was buried in the Bennington Village Cemetery.

PATSY SANTO

1893–1975

Pasquale "Patsy" Santo was a local housepainter who became nationally known as an artist. He was born in Corsano, a small town at the tip of the heel of Italy, on Christmas Day 1893. Santo worked as a woodcarver in Italy until 1913, when he immigrated to America, promising his mother he would return in a year. It was more than fifty years later that he made his first trip back to Italy. In America, he held a variety of jobs with companies like the Delaware and Hudson Railroad, the Warner Brush Company, the Holden Leonard Company and the E-Z Mills, and then he became a house painter full time. Not only did he paint several pictures of the Old First Church, but he also painted the church itself. He married Irene White of Greenwich, New York, in 1917, had two children and settled on Dewey Street in Bennington for most of his adult life

Santo took up painting as a hobby in 1923, when he made pictures and decorations for family and friends to decorate their walls. He painted a mural for a North Street shoe repair shop on commission, but it wasn't until 1937 that he ventured to exhibit his work publicly. He entered a painting in the Rutland State Fair and won first prize. There, Walt Kuhn, the organizer of the famous Armory Show that introduced modern European art to America, discovered Patsy's work and encouraged him to develop his own "Modern Primitive" style. The following year, Santo showed three paintings at the Southern Vermont Artists Association in Manchester, and in 1939, he had his first big break when he was included in the Museum of Modern Art's *Contemporary Unknown American Artists* exhibit in New York City. The museum

Ready for Battle, painting by Patsy Santo, 1954. *Bennington Museum, Bennington, VT.*

purchased one of his works for its permanent collection. Art historian and director of the Williams College Museum of Art Lane Faison wrote that Santo's work displayed an "authentic innocent eye." His work is much more technically accomplished than the region's other famous primitive, Grandma Moses, and his more realistic Bennington area scenes are highly prized by local collectors. It is interesting to note that his harshest criticism came from the *Bennington Banner*, his hometown newspaper. In October 1940, it ran a long article about his work, in which it debunked the idea that he was a "Romantic primitive." They pointed out that instead of being self-taught, he had received a good deal of artistic training before he left Italy and that it was a false statement to call him a primitive. "What one feels in Santo's work as a whole is a lack of originality of creative composition," the critic wrote. Many of his collectors would disagree.

Unlike most folk artists, Santo's paintings show a constant stylistic development and improvement in the way he depicts local themes. In his book *They Taught Themselves*, art collector and gallery owner Sidney Janis points out the skill and understanding Santo used in depicting his subjects.

Early on, his exhibits sold out in important New York City galleries, such as the Marie Harriman Gallery and the Macbeth Gallery.

Since Patsy's discovery, many museums and galleries have exhibited Santo's paintings. In addition to the Museum of Modern Art, these institutions include the Whitney Museum of American Art, the Corcoran Gallery, the Metropolitan Museum of Art and, of course, the Bennington Museum. Well-known private collectors and celebrities, such as Mrs. Vincent Astor, Mrs. Paul Mellon, Mrs. Payne Whitney, Raymond Loewy, Lillian Hellman, Helen Hayes and Hedy Lamarr, have also purchased his work. Santo died in Bennington on May 10, 1975; he was buried in the Park Lawn Cemetery.

NORMAN ROCKWELL AND HIS MODELS

1894–1978

When Norman Rockwell and his family moved to Arlington, Vermont, in 1939, the change affected the artist's work, as well as his life. Many of the models he hired there had strong ties to Bennington through family and friends, and a number of them still lived and worked there. Over the course of Rockwell's next fifteen years in Vermont, models and scenes from the Bennington area came to represent a vision of small-town America at its best. One example of this is found in his 1953 painting *Walking to Church*. The scene of a young family on their way to Sunday services is a composite that shows a restaurant building in Troy, a barbershop in Cambridge and, in the background, the steeple of the First Baptist Church in Bennington.

Rockwell and his second wife, Mary Barstow, moved to Arlington from New York City, where Norman had been born and educated. By the time he made his decision to move to Vermont, Rockwell was a successful illustrator best known for his covers for the *Saturday Evening Post*. Beginning early as a professional, he had won his first commercial contract in 1912 at the age of eighteen, a series of pictures for a book titled *Tell Me Why Stories*, for which he was paid $150. He soon became a regular illustrator for *Boys' Life* and eventually many other publications. By the end of his career, he would be credited with some two hundred *Post* covers, as well as hundreds of other illustrations for posters, cards and advertisements.

Rockwell's life was not entirely what one might imagine from the scenes of innocent rural and suburban life he produced. Rockwell and his first wife, Irene O'Connor, had sought to live an upscale life in the suburbs of New

Norman Rockwell and Grandma Moses cutting her birthday cake. *Bennington Museum, Bennington, VT.*

York City. But by the late 1930s, Rockwell had tired of dining in country and yacht clubs with executives from the Edison, Coca-Cola and Hallmark companies. He found that his work was not as personally rewarding as he imagined. After an unsuccessful trip to Europe in search of his artistic roots, he eventually moved to Arlington, a town he found on the advice of one of his models who enjoyed fishing on the Battenkill.

Rockwell liked Arlington and the Bennington region. It was rural but still relatively close to New York, the center for publishing and illustration. At that time, it was a stop on the regular passenger rail route and had nearby Bennington College for intellectual stimulation. The area's Revolutionary War history, with its raucous Green Mountain Boys and a legacy of resistance to authority, also appealed to Rockwell. Here, he found other artists and writers who had chosen the area as their own home, including Carl Ruggles, Reginald Marsh, Rockwell Kent, Dorothy Canfield Fisher and Robert Frost.

The principal change for Rockwell, as he described it in his autobiography, *Norman Rockwell: My Adventures as Illustrator*, was that in Arlington, he began to work not with professional models but with local models and made scenes drawn from the community around him. This gave his art a more direct link to the subject of the American spirit that was central to his work. It melded the Rockwells into a community in which they felt comfortable, and the citizens of Bennington County came to play an important chapter in American art.

Among Rockwell's paintings from his Arlington period were a spate of *Saturday Evening Post* covers and a number of images tied specifically to World War II and to the depiction of American values. Many of the images of this period featured local models. Thus, Mary Immen, later Mary Immen Hall, who frequently modeled for Rockwell, became a child being rescued from a flood by brave Boy Scout Horace Young, while Marjorie and Larry Brush and their children became the family consulting the quintessential country doctor, Arlington's Dr. George Russell. Bob Buck, a sawmill worker from Rupert whom Rockwell encountered at local Grange dances, became the model for a popular series based on the character Willie Gillis, the artist's idea of the ideal army recruit, and Arlington's Carl Hess, who later worked for the North Bennington Polygraphic Company, represented the unforgettable image of an American speaking out at town meeting, the Freedom of Speech image from Rockwell's Four Freedoms. Once again near the mid-point of the twentieth century, Bennington citizens became models of American freedom and spirit, just as they had some 150 years earlier at the Battle of Bennington.

NORTON BARBER

1903–1983

Like others of his generation, Norton Barber, attorney, public servant and active citizen of Bennington for many years, bridged a time of change between two very different eras. The aplomb with which he navigated those years endeared him to many and left a lasting impression on the people who knew him.

After he was born in Bennington in 1903, Barber's family moved to Washington, D.C., when he was six, as his father had been appointed an appeals judge for the United States Customs Service. Barber attended school in Washington and later graduated from Exeter and Harvard. In 1928, he completed two years at Harvard Law School. Returning to Bennington, he undertook a clerkship and became a member of the Vermont bar in 1929.

Barber's long career began during Prohibition, when he served as state's attorney to Bennington County. Among his early controversial cases, one involved prosecuting a local judge for showing a movie on Sunday. Though he won the approbation of the clergymen who had encouraged him, he later admitted that the matter had occasioned him considerable personal distress.

The list of the many offices Barber held in the town and state is very long. In 1939, 1941 and 1943, he was elected as the town's representative to the legislature, and in 1945, he was made a state senator. In service to his profession, he was president of the Vermont Bar Association and served on its board of examiners for twenty-five years. He was also a trustee of the University of Vermont and member of the state's board of education.

Barber's best-known public roles were local. First elected in 1943, he remained town moderator until his death forty years later in 1983. He was also the town's attorney for more than thirty years. Known as an authority on municipal law in the state, he was the important force behind the drafting of the town's Consolidation Act of 1970. That act allowed for the merging of the Villages of Bennington, Old Bennington and North Bennington, which ushered in a new era for the local government.

Norton married Marcia Stevens from Hoosick Falls on September 10, 1932, and together, they raised a family in Bennington. She was as active as her husband. Over her nearly ninety-eight years of life, she devoted herself to church work, garden clubs and the League of Women Voters, at the same time serving on the Vermont Natural Resources Council and other environmental commissions. During the 1960s, she helped pass the legislation that banned roadside billboards throughout the state.

What many remember about Norman Barber was his firm self-image as an attorney. Marshall Witten of Bennington, a young associate during the latter portion of Barber's career, was impressed by Barber's lawyerly appearance and demeanor. He recalls Barber with his thumbs in his suspenders, tilted back in an old wooden office chair, peering inquiringly under his wire-rimmed glasses. Speaking in a personal pattern of rhythms and expressions, he projected the affect of a country lawyer. Nonetheless, added Witten, behind the impression of relaxation was the experienced graduate of Exeter and Harvard who could help guide a private consultation or a public meeting toward a productive end.

Attorney and Williams College professor Harvey Carter, who clerked for Barber early in his own career, remembered Barber's professional and highly practiced manner. While working for Barber in his offices at 469 Main Street, Carter benefited from his wisdom, even while enduring some sharp criticism. "It was another era," recalled Witten, "a different kind of practice. It recalls a time that was more nuanced, and perceptive, and in which our view of the law and its practice was more inclusive."

Many remember Barber's directness and generosity, unusual qualities for a man who often put his public and professional work first. Today, we are certainly beneficiaries of his long tenure in local affairs and can perhaps learn from the qualities he brought to them.

JANE RICHARDSON HANKS

1908–2014

Not many people live to be 100 years old, but anthropologist Jane Hanks lived to be nearly 106. She was born Jane Richardson in Berkeley, California, on August 2, 1908, the daughter of a Latin professor at the University of California. As a student, she attended college at Berkeley, where she received her degree in 1930 before going on to Columbia University for her graduate work. While at Berkeley, she was encouraged by a professor named Alfred Kroeber to study ethnology and anthropology. Kroeber and Richardson teamed up to study the changes in women's dress styles over the years, and in 1940, they published their findings in an influential study called *Three Centuries of Women's Dress Fashions: A Quantitative Analysis*. One thing that it discovered was that the length of women's skirts was related to the national economy.

After moving to New York in 1936, she studied with Ruth Benedict, a close associate of Margaret Mead, and found her own true calling as an anthropologist. Her field work took her to Oklahoma to study the culture of the Kiowa Indians with her teacher Alexander Lesser, and that resulted in a dissertation titled "Law and Status Among the Kiowa." She finished her research work and passed her doctoral defense in 1938 but did not officially receive her doctorate until 1943, due to a paperwork snafu. She maintained her interest in the Kiowa and Blackfoot tribes for the rest of her career.

It was while working in the field with Abraham Maslow on a study of the Blackfoot Indians of Canada that she met her future husband, psychologist

Jane Hanks. *Courtesy of the* Bennington Banner.

Lucien "June" Hanks Jr., who was also interested in anthropology. In 1938, they were married, and together, they had three children over the next few years. Like so many women of that era, she put aside her career in order to raise her children. She described her professional work as being split into two periods, "before children and after children." As further evidence of the unique problems women had to face when seeking professional employment is a letter of recommendation that Professor Kroeber wrote for Hanks when she was seeking employment with the WPA Federal Writers' Project in 1935. She was not seeking a job as an anthropologist but a job as a writer. Kroeber pointed out that since she probably wouldn't be able to get a job as an anthropologist because of her sex, he'd be willing to give her up. "Only reason I'd let you tempt her…is that she's a woman and therefore a regular anthropological career is uncertain for her," he wrote.

In 1942, June was appointed to the faculty at Bennington College, and the family settled on Pleasant Street in North Bennington. From then on, Jane and June collaborated on much of their anthropological research, becoming experts in the cultures of Southeast Asia after Lucien's wartime assignments in Burma. This work, beginning in 1944, resulted in several books, including *Tribes of the North Thailand Frontier* and *Maternity and Its Rituals in Bang Chan.* In the 1960s, their fieldwork included long periods spent in the hill towns of northern Thailand, where Jane Hanks served as a consultant for the Peace Corps.

In addition to mentoring and lecturing at Bennington College, SUNY Albany and Williams, Jane pursued other activities. Jane was a woman of diverse interests, and while living in North Bennington, she took an active role in the community by working to preserve the Park-McCullough House and played violin with the Sage City Symphony. She and June also founded the Sage City Syndicate in order to preserve the character of the village by buying and renovating old houses in the area.

In 2002, at the age of ninety-four, June won the Distinguished Contributions to Asian Studies Award, which is given by the Association for Asian Studies. Jane was also recognized for her many contributions to her hometown in 2006, when North Bennington declared August 6 Jane Hanks Day. She died on July 27, 2014, in her home on Hillside Street, where she had lived for several decades.

PAULINE LEADER

1908–2001

Although Pauline Leader was born in New York City, she grew up in Bennington. As soon as she came of age, she moved back to the city of her birth and proceeded to write a scathing memoir about her childhood in Vermont. The book, *And No Birds Sing*, paints an unattractive picture of the people she knew and the experiences she had in Bennington, and it describes in grim detail the many trials she suffered here. Many people in Bennington didn't like the way she portrayed the town, while others sympathized with her plight.

Pauline was born into a poor Jewish immigrant family on October 16, 1908. Her father, Isaac Leader, had recently come to America from Ukraine. Her mother, Frieda Kovensky Leader, was from Belarus and worked in her husband's butcher shop, the Cut Price Market on North Street. The family lived in two dark, dingy rooms in the same building as the shop. In those days, Jewish businesses were discouraged from opening on Main Street, so most were located on North Street, near Pleasant Street. The customers of the Cut Price were mainly other immigrants who worked in the local mills. Pauline hated the meat market; it smelled, and she couldn't get away from it. Her mother, whom she pities in the book, worked there all day, every day. She hated her father for making her mother work so hard, lifting sides of beef and doing all the dirty work. Isaac also became Bennington's first rabbi in 1923, so he could escape to the Congregation Beth El meeting rooms in the Noveck Block whenever he needed a break. This contributed to Pauline's hatred of Judaism, which she displays in her work. Because of her alienation, Pauline became an outsider in every sense of the word.

Pauline Leader, 1957. *Bennington Museum, Bennington, VT.*

In April 1921, when Leader was twelve years old, she lost her hearing after a bout with spinal meningitis. The doctor believed that she would recover her hearing, but she did not. By coincidence, her illness came in the same week that she learned she had received very high marks in school, 97 percent. From then on, she was unable to hear her teachers and was expelled for not following instructions. Her mother refused to send her to school to learn how to read lips, so Pauline depended on herself for the rest of her education. She read at the public library, watched movies and wrote poetry. She also escaped from the meat market to hang around the train station, where she enjoyed the company of the alcoholic bums and the unemployed men. Often, she was beaten for her absences and locked in the family's apartment. As a child, she was disciplined and abused, and after she left school, she had to go to work in a factory at the age of fourteen. By all reports, she was a defiant, spiteful child.

When the meat market closed, her father converted a large house nearby into small apartments and built two larger boardinghouses on the same block near the corner of Pleasant and School Streets. Today, you might call these cheap rooms a flophouse. It was known as the Leader Block, and although it started out fresh and new, it soon became the hub of a seedier part of town. Many people have memories of the poverty, sex work and drugs that abounded here.

Just before she turned eighteen, with twenty dollars she had hidden away, Leader ran away from home and headed straight for Greenwich Village in New York City. The restrictive nature of small-town life had become too much for her to bear. She quickly settled into the Bohemian life of the Village, made friends and wrote poems and stories between shifts working in factories and sweatshops. The harsh conditions of her working-class life led her to become involved with communist and socialist politics. In 1928, two of her poems were published in the prestigious magazine *Poetry*, as well as some other literary publications. In 1931, her first book, *And No Birds Sing*, was published by Vanguard to great acclaim, although the sales never matched its positive reviews. Ethel Mannin called the book "a terrible indictment of the social system and the moral code." Of course, the local review in the *Bennington Evening Banner* noted that the book "will not be appreciated by them [Bennington folk] but it may be a lesson to them."

While in Greenwich Village, Leader met and married the writer Millen Brand and had several children with him. His 1937 book *The Outward Room* is a psychological thriller whose heroine's life closely resembles Leader's. He also wrote scripts for a number of plays and movies, most famously that of *The Snake Pit* in 1948. Then in 1953, Millen was officially blacklisted when he refused to name names before Senator Joseph McCarthy's House Un-American Activities Committee.

Pauline raised her two sons, Daniel and Jonathan, alone after her 1942 divorce from Brand. Her memories of this period were the basis for her second book, *A Room for the Night*. It details the inhabitants of her mother's boardinghouse, remembered here as the Leader House. It is interesting that Pauline never turned her back on Bennington, even though she wrote so much about her hard times here. Her mother died at the age of thirty-nine shortly after Pauline ran away, and then in 1934, her father passed away. After her parents' deaths, she returned again and again to visit her siblings and eventually moved back to live in Bennington for the rest of her life. She never wrote another book, but her letters to the editor were often published in the pages of the *Bennington Banner*. Sadly, she did not achieve lasting success as a writer, and her books have been all but forgotten. She died in 2001.

SHIRLEY JACKSON

1916–1965

Bennington College brought a new level of prestige to the Bennington area through the faculty, speakers and artists who were attracted to the school. Hand in hand with this was the presence of the spouses, children and associates of the teaching professionals. From the late 1940s to the mid-1960s, one of North Bennington's best-known citizens was the writer Shirley Jackson, wife of Bennington College faculty member Stanley Edgar Hyman. She was the author of the celebrated short story "The Lottery."

Born in San Francisco on December 14, 1916, and educated in Upstate New York, Jackson had written poetry and prose from an early age. She and her husband met at Syracuse University while they were working on the school's literary magazine. It was the first of many controversial enterprises in which they were involved.

Though fully appreciative of the formal education she received, Jackson said that her real education came from a year she took off from college. During that self-imposed hiatus, she read and wrote regularly and developed the creative habits that would enable her to produce a steady stream of popular stories, articles and novels. This discipline lasted until her early death in 1965, when she was just forty-eight.

What set Jackson apart from other writers was her ability to tell a story. It enabled her to translate both her experiences and imagination into compelling and interesting tales, and her lean toward all things magical, spiritual and mysterious lent a unique tone of psychological suspense to her

Shirley Jackson, 1947. *Bennington Museum, Bennington, VT.*

work. To this was added a sense of morality and fairness that appealed to many readers.

By 1945, when the Hymans arrived in North Bennington from New York, Jackson had already begun to establish herself as a serious writer. In 1941, her first national publication, the humorous story "My Life with R.H. Macy," based on her interim work with that firm, was published in *The New Republic*. In 1943, she published the first of her many stories for *The New Yorker*, and in 1944, her "Come Dance With Me in Ireland" was chosen for the annual volume *Best American Short Stories*.

But it was with "The Lottery" that Jackson made her mark. This haunting tale set in a small New England town brought the echoes of Puritan madness and intolerance associated with witchcraft into the present. Its publication in 1948 marked Jackson's transformation from a quietly aspiring writer to a national figure and the focus of considerable discussion and debate. Though she had published several stories that year, as well as her first novel, it was "The Lottery," with its critical view of communities and the ostensibly normal citizens who inhabited them, on which the public focused. "Could people really be so different than they appeared to be?" they asked. Indeed, this observation turned out to be the basis of much of Jackson's work.

Aside from the many letters she received, "The Lottery" had other effects on Jackson's marketability and notoriety. In 1952, Jackson produced almost a story per month for popular magazines like *Collier's*, *Harper's* and *Good Housekeeping*. That same year, "The Lottery" was adapted for television, the new medium of the day. A year later, Jackson published ten additional stories and a new book. It was also in 1953 that "The Lottery" was adapted to the stage and became one of the most regularly performed one-act plays in the nation. In 1956, Jackson's third novel, *The Bird's Nest*, written in 1954, was adapted to become the movie *Lizzie*, starring Eleanor Parker, Richard Boone and Joan Blondell.

For the next decade of her professional life, Jackson continued to be very productive. In addition to her writing career, she and her husband raised four children in North Bennington. Some of their experiences formed the basis of numerous published articles and her two humorous books that chronicled her family life here, *Life Among the Savages* (1953) and *Raising Demons* (1957). Until 1965, the Hymans continued to lead a spirited and agreeably unconventional life in North Bennington. They were devoted to sports and games and were serious readers. Their family library, with some thirty thousand volumes, was probably larger than that of the college.

Perhaps Bennington College faculty member Howard Nemerov, later Poet Laureate of the United States, best evoked Jackson's collegial but combative spirit in a tribute to her that was written shortly after her death in 1965: "'My friends,' Chekhov said, looking in at a party, 'you live badly.'" Nemerov quoted. "Shirley Jackson, too," he continued, himself, "has told us with great brilliance and strength that we live badly; but she has always said to us also, 'My friends'!"

Jackson died in her sleep on August 8, 1965, at her home in North Bennington.

DAVID GIL

1922–2002

Bennington's most recent contribution to the field of ceramics is the popular company called Bennington Potters, located on County Street. Though not directly connected to its earlier forebears, it carries on the tradition of being a commercially viable producer of fine ceramics in a town that has been associated with pottery for more than two centuries.

When David Gil and his wife, Gloria, arrived in Bennington in 1948, they could hardly have known that their fledgling pottery business would survive for more than seventy-five years and become an important economic base in the region. Gil and Gloria, who saw themselves more as artists than businesspeople, would certainly have been surprised to know that a half century later, in 1974 and 1977, Gil would be named Businessman of the Year, first by the U.S. Small Business Agency and later by the State of Vermont. His commercial skills may have originated with his father, who ran a commercial business of his own.

David Gil, born David Goldfarb in 1922, grew up in New York City and graduated from Alfred University in Upstate New York, where he earned his degree in ceramics. As a young man during World War II, he served as a radio operator in the merchant marine. Arriving in Bennington after the war with a few thousand dollars that he had saved from his days in the merchant marine, Gil set up shop in a barn that had recently been converted into a pottery by Edgar Johnson on McCall Street. Originally called Cooperative Design, the company renamed itself the Bennington Potters Inc.

David Gil's signature trigger mug.
Bennington Museum, Bennington, VT.

For some dozen years, Gil's pottery, as well as his personal life, operated from that site, as he often traveled to market his wares himself. In 1960, after a fire in the pottery, the business was moved to the rented buildings the company still occupies, the old Henry W. Myers Grist Mill. Gil later purchased the complex, originally built around 1896, which, under his guidance over the years, contained a variety of small businesses complementary to his own. The key to the pottery's success has been its steadily changing yet remarkably consistent line of ceramic goods, which combine sophisticated basic designs with a usefulness and simplicity shoppers find hard to resist. Some of Gil's most successful designs, his "trigger" mugs, for example, and playful small objects from trivets and ashtrays to candlesticks and figurines, have been copied by others, but the Bennington Potters' commitment to unpretentious design and to a production process that preserves the esthetic values of handmade crafts, has kept buyers returning. Gil himself passed away in 2002, but the business carries on.

From a practical point of view, the Bennington Potters is a great success. Drawing clay by the ton from Ohio, New York, Georgia, Tennessee and other locations, its combination of hand crafting and judicious automation have continued to make its production and sales grow. It is a major local employer in town, and its workers produce a large number of plates, cups, pitchers and casseroles yearly from hundreds of separate designs. The products of the pottery are of such high quality that they have been displayed in museums and galleries as well as retail shops across the country. In 2023, in honor of what would have been David Gil's one hundredth birthday, the Bennington Museum mounted a huge retrospective of his work. In addition to Gil's commercial work, the company has seen the periodic production of artists' pieces by the likes of Leonard Baskin and David Smith and ceramic panels for murals by other artists, among them Romare Bearden, Larry Rivers and Bennington College graduate Helen Frankenthaler. The Bennington Potters remains under the direction of Gil's second wife, Sheela Harden, a recent chapter in Bennington's long association with ceramics.

PAULA WELDEN

1928–DISAPPEARED 1946

The case of Paula Jean Welden, an eighteen-year-old Bennington College student who disappeared inexplicably in 1946, has intrigued Benningtonians ever since. Despite the numerous mysteries and unanswered questions surrounding the case, it has at least one positive, if surprising, outcome: the founding of the Vermont State Police.

When Paula Welden, a Bennington sophomore from Stamford, Connecticut, left the Bennington College campus on December 1, 1946, she told her friends that she simply intended to take a hike on Mount Anthony. She dressed lightly for a December day; did not take any extra clothing, supplies or money; and refused a ride from passing friends. It did not seem like she was on her way to anywhere in particular. Yet after receiving a ride from a stranger, not to Mount Anthony but to the site of the Long Trail in Woodford, the attractive coed disappeared completely, never to be seen again.

On finding she had not yet returned to her room on the morning of December 2, Paula's roommate contacted the college's administration. When Paula was still not back by noon, the president of the college was notified. He called Paula's parents to see if she had gone home. Later in the day, the Bennington County state's attorney and Sheriff Clyde Peck were contacted. A search party was organized, but nothing was found.

Later information from the driver who had offered her a ride moved the search for Paula to the Woodford area, the Long Trail and Glastenbury Mountain. Hundreds of searchers spent days hunting for signs of Welden's

Paula Welden. *Courtesy of the* Bennington Banner.

whereabouts. Outside experts were brought in, a helicopter was employed and an investigation that lasted some weeks ensued. Paula's father, a wealthy industrial engineer, consulted the renowned psychic from Pownal Clara Jepson. Not one to be taken lightly, Mrs. Jepson had been consulted about lost persons by the Lindberghs and the husband of Amelia Earhart. She was noted in her obituary in the *Banner*, some thirty years afterward, to have been awarded "the highest rating of clairvoyants" and a certificate of merit by the Rockefeller Foundation. Perhaps not coincidentally, she successfully located a $2,000 diamond pin for a resident of Old Bennington, a daughter of John D. Rockefeller. Mrs. Jepson announced that Paula was still alive and would be found in an abandoned shack.

Under these circumstances and conditions, theories about the disappearance of Paula Welden flourished. Some believed she had died by suicide. Others, noting that she was not the first disappearance in the area, suggested that she had been murdered. (A lumberman had vanished nearby the year before.) A third theory, based on circumstances of the time—disagreements with her parents, depression and a possible liaison with a member of the opposite sex—suggested that she may not have entered the woods at all but fled along the highway to a tryst or a new life elsewhere.

Because she has never been heard from again, the most logical theory would seem to be that Welden, intentionally or unintentionally, became lost in the woods. It was late in the day when she set out. She had only light clothing and no money or supplies. It snowed that night, and it would have been difficult for her to be comfortable or even safe.

The inability of authorities and volunteers to find any trace of Paula Welden has given the case its lasting significance. The investigation was disorganized, and no one, not the college, the public or Welden's family, was satisfied. Most agreed that an informal search by volunteers, somewhat after the fact and coordinated by a sheriff who had recently been voted out of office by a disgruntled electorate, was inadequate. On July 1, 1947, in response to the trauma surrounding the Welden case, a corps of officers was formed to provide professional statewide oversight in important cases: the Vermont State Police.

Theories about Paula Welden's whereabouts continue. A 1976 article written for the *Banner* by Tim Powers, whose parents had been peripherally involved in the case, noted that Welden was believed by some to be still alive and roaming the woods in Glastenbury. It has also been suggested that she might have been mystically transported to another world. These are fascinating speculations and place Welden in a category of missing persons along with Amelia Earhart, Judge Crater and Jimmy Hoffa.

BENNINGTON COLLEGE

FOUNDED 1932

Bennington College is included as a general topic here due to the vast number of people who have visited, taught and stayed at the college over the years. A select list of notable people associated with the college is all that can be given here. Full biographies would require an entire book in itself, and they are easily available elsewhere. The idea for the school was first proposed in 1923 by Reverend Vincent Ravi Booth, the pastor of the Old First Church and the subject of a biography earlier in this book. Since the school's first classes were held, many celebrated people have come to the area and called Bennington their home for short or long periods.

Booth felt that if a college was established here, it would help bolster church attendance, which usually flagged during the winter. For the planning stage, he was able to convince several people to support his idea; Mr. and Mrs. Hall Park McCullough, Mr. and Mrs. James Colgate, Paul Moody and William Heard Kilpatrick, a progressive educator, all gave their advice. Robert Devore Leigh, who had been a professor at Williams College, agreed to become the first president of the college, an office he held from 1928 to 1941. Mrs. McCullough also helped gather the team of progressive educators who came up with the school's modern, forward-looking approach to college education for women. The concept was that teaching would be done by practitioners in various fields, not by professional educators. As a result, literature was taught by writers, art was taught by painters and sculptors and music was taught by musicians and composers. It was a simple formula that made Bennington College unique. In 1932, the first class of eighty-seven students arrived.

Early days at Bennington College. *Bennington Museum, Bennington, VT.*

Over the years, a legion of prominent figures from every field imaginable have come to Bennington. A short list of teachers from the past three-quarters of a century must include writers like W.H. Auden, Ben Belitt, John Gardner, Stanley Kunitz, Bernard Malamud, Howard Nemerov, Mary Oliver, Theodore Roethke and Stephen Sandy; artists like Buckminster Fuller, Kenneth Noland, Jules Olitski and David Smith; composers and musicians like Henry Brant, Bill Dixon, Paul Feeley and Allen Shawn; dancers like Viola Farber, Martha Graham, Martha Hill and José Limón; and critics like Kenneth Burke, Clement Greenberg and Stanley Hyman. The tradition continues to this day.

BIBLIOGRAPHY

Aldrich, Lewis Cass. *History of Bennington County, Vermont.* D. Mason & Co., 1889.

Allen, Ethan. *Reason: The Only Oracle of Man.* Haswell, 1785.

Allen, Ira. *The Natural and Political History of the State of Vermont.* Tuttle, 1984.

Beers, F.W. *Atlas of Bennington County Vermont.* Beers, 1869.

Benedict, G.G. *Vermont in the Civil War.* 2 vols. The Free Press Association, 1888.

Benjamin, Asher. *The Country Builder's Assistant.* Thomas Dickman, 1797.

Bennington Banner (various issues)

Bennington Historical Society and Bennington Museum. *Bennington.* Images of America. Arcadia Publishing, 2002.

Brockway, Thomas P. *Bennington College: In the Beginning.* Bennington College Press, 1981.

Burleigh, Lucien. *Bennington, Vermont.* Burleigh Lithograph Co., 1887.

Bushnell, Mark. *Hidden History of Vermont.* The History Press, 2017.

Conant, Edward. *Geography, History and Civil Government of Vermont.* Tuttle Co., 1890.

Cox, Belinda J., et al. "The Cloverleaf Site." *Journal of Vermont Archaeology* 3 (2000): 17–32.

Crockett, Walter Hill. *Vermont: The Green Mountain State.* 3 vols. Century History Co., 1921.

Day Papers. Bennington Museum Library. Bennington, VT.

Fay, Glenn, Jr. *Vermont's Ebenezer Allen.* The History Press, 2021.

Fels, Tom. *Poets & Pioneers, 50 Lives in the History of Bennington.* Bennington Bicenquinquagenary, 1999.

Fisher, Dorothy Canfield. *The Brimming Cup.* Harcourt, Brace and Co., 1921.

———. *Memories of Arlington, Vermont.* Duell, Sloan and Pearce, 1921.

Franklin, Ruth. *Shirley Jackson: A Rather Haunted Life.* Norton, 2016.

Gabriel, Michael P. *The Battle of Bennington: Soldiers & Civilians.* The History Press, 2012.

Hall, Joseph H. *Bygone Bennington.* Inkspot Press, n.d.

Hanks, Jane Richardson. *Maternity and Its Rituals in Bang Chan.* Cornell University, 1963.

———. *Three Centuries of Women's Dress Fashions.* Hassell Street Press, 2021.

———. *Tribes of the North Thailand Frontier.* Yale University Press, 2001.

Harmon, Daniel Williams. *A Journal of Voyages and Travels in the Interior of North America.* Flagg and Gould, 1820.

Hubbard, Eleanor. "Vermont's Underground Railroad." *Vermont Historical Society Bulletin* 33, no. 2 (April 1965): 308–12.

Jackson, Shirley. *Life Among the Savages.* Farrar, Straus and Young, 1953.

———. *The Lottery.* Farrar, Straus and Co., 1949.

———. *Raising Demons.* Farrar, Straus and Cudahy, 1957.

Jennings, Isaac. *Memorials of a Century.* Gould and Lincoln, 1869.

Leader, Pauline. *And No Birds Sing.* Gallaudet University Press, 2016.

———. *A Room for the Night.* Vanguard Press, 1946.

Levin, Ruth. *Ordinary Heroes: The Story of Shaftsbury, Vermont.* Shaftsbury Historical Society, 1990.

Mello, Robert A. *Moses Robinson and the Founding of Vermont.* Vermont Historical Society, 2014.

Millen, Brand. *The Outward Room.* Simon and Schuster, 1933.

Morgan, Bill. *Bennington and the Civil War.* The History Press, 2013.

Murray, Stuart. *Norman Rockwell at Home in Vermont.* Images from the Past, 1997.

Niles, Grace Greylock. *The Hoosac Valley: Its Legends and Its History.* G.P. Putnam & Sons, 1912.

Oneal, Zibby. *Grandma Moses: Painter of Rural America.* Puffin Books, 1987.

Randall, Willard Sterne. *Ethan Allen: Life and Times.* Norton, 2011.

Resch, Tyler. *Bennington's Battle Monument: Massive and Lofty.* Images from the Past, 1993.

———. *Deed of Gift.* Paradigm Press, 1991.

———, ed. *The Shires of Bennington.* Bennington Banner, 1975.

Robinson, Melvin H., ed. *Bennington Souvenir 1904.* YMCA, 1904.

Rose, Ben Z. *John Stark: Maverick General.* TreeLine Press, 2007.

Rural Vermont: A Program for the Future. Vermont Commission on Country Life, 1931.

Scheetz, Thomas. *An Updated History of Buildings in Old Bennington: 1761–1012.* Privately printed, 2023.

Shalhope, Robert E. *A Tale of New England.* John Hopkins University Press, 2003.

Sherman, Michael, et al. *Freedom and Unity: A History of Vermont.* Vermont Historical Society, 2004.

Smith, Richard B. *The Revolutionary War in Bennington County: A History & Guide.* The History Press, 2008.

Spargo, John. *The Bennington Battle Monument: Its Story and Its Meaning.* Tuttle, 1925.

———. *The Potters and Potteries of Bennington.* Houghton Mifflin, 1926.

———. *The Story of David Redding Who Was Hanged.* Bennington Historical Museum and Art Gallery, 1945.

Stewart, Almira Doty. "Diary." Unpublished manuscript in the collection of the University of Vermont, 1901.

Stone, Arthur F. *The Vermont of Today.* Lewis Historical Publishing Co., 1929.

Ullery, Jacob G. *Men of Vermont.* Transcript Publishing Co., 1894.

Vermonters: A Book of Biographies. Stephen Daye Press, 1932.

Vermont Quarterly Gazetteer no. 2 (1861).

Walbridge, Herbert Stebbins. *The History and Development of North Bennington Vermont.* N.p., 1937.

Whitfield, Harvey Amani. *The Problem of Slavery in Early Vermont, 1777–1810.* Vermont Historical Society, 2014.

Wills, Hazel McLeod. *Bill Wills and Company.* Privately printed, 1953.

Zirblis, Raymond Paul. *Friends of Freedom: The Vermont Underground Railroad Survey Report.* Vermont Department of State Buildings and Vermont Division for Historic Preservation, 1996.

Zusy, Catherine. *Norton Stoneware and American Redware: The Bennington Museum Collection.* Bennington Museum, 1991.

Zwicker, Roxie J. *Vermont Book of the Dead.* The History Press, 2023.

ABOUT THE AUTHORS

Bill Morgan is an author, archivist and bibliographer living in Bennington. He has written more than forty books dealing with history and literature, including *I Celebrate Myself: The Somewhat Private Life of Allen Ginsberg* (Viking Press) and *The Typewriter Is Holy: The Complete Uncensored History of the Beat Generation* (Simon & Schuster). He currently serves as the secretary of the Bennington Historical Society.

Tom Fels is a curator and writer based in North Bennington whose exhibitions have been shown at the Getty Museum in Malibu and the Van Gogh Museum in Amsterdam. He is the author of numerous books and articles on topics ranging from nineteenth-century photography to the nature of contemporary counterculture and the history of Bennington.